SOME NOTES ABOUT PST TOMOWO···

'Pastor Adetomowo Faduyile George, I have a rare opportunity to read through some of your books on Christian religious topics. I am amazed by the high level of research into the words of God as revealed in your well articulated, inspiring and redeeming books. At a stage, I became confused if the write-up could have emanated from a pharmacist with little or no bias to Christian religion. The topic and soul winning books authored by a Princess of a Prominent Traditional Ruler in whose palace, traditional, Christian, and other religious practices compete, I hesitate not in recommending to all and sundry the books for reading and studying to witness how God works.'

- His Royal Majesty, Oba Alayeluwa George Babatunde Faduyile,
The Abodi of Ikaleland, Ondo State, Nigeria.

'Pastor tomowo is a trained consultant pharmacist who is fervent for the Lord. Her burning desire to reach people across geographical borders of nations through the Church in the Air has blessed many homes and individuals. May our Lord prosper her Vision and continually renew her Anointing.'

- Dr Kayode Afolabi,
Consultant Obstetrician and Gynaecologist,
Director, Reproductive Health, Federal Ministry of Health, Abuja, Nigeria

'Pastor Tomowo, my very close friend and sister, is my most spiritual female friend grounded in the ways and acts of God. I know undoubtedly that she does not only have God but knows and walk with Him intimately –and unto this, she's sold out. She lives a life of wholeness both on and off the pulpit'.

- Dr Oyinbo Manuel,
Resident Pastor, Kingsway International Christian Centre,
Windhoek, Namibia.

'Pastor Tomowo is... A true lover of the Lord Jesus. Passionate about the kingdom of God. Committed to enlightening saints with the Truth of Christ'.

- Pastor Bankie Olusina.
Kingdom –Word Ministries,
Enugu, Nigeria.

'I have known Pst Tomowo for about 3 years, and most of our interactions have been online... In about this time I have come to identify Pst Tomowo as one with a heart and passion for the Word of God...
I have noticed she more often than not has a balanced take on the Word which is one major reason I keep reading her articles and sometimes listen to her podcasts... She strikes me as humble with a heart that values relationship and the unity of the Spirit in the bond of peace'...

- Dr Faith Ekpekurede
Coordinator, God's Kept women Intl.
and Member, Board of Trustee CUNAA UK/Europe,
Kent, United Kingdom.

'I have known pastor tomowo for almost two years now. She loves God very dearly, and she has a very good understanding of God's Word that she teaches weekly. Focusing on contemporary topics and issues that are relevant to the needs of believers hungry for the Truth of God's Word and how to apply that Truth in living out the Christian life victoriously in the 21st century".

- Gabriel Okougha
Resident Pastor, KICC, The Fountain of Grace,
Gray, Essex, London, United Kingdom

THE 3RD PERSON IN MARRIAGE SERIES. . .

THE CHOOSING

Focusing on making the right choice for Marriage!

The 3rd Person in Marriage

series...

THE CHOOSING

The Church in the Air.

pst tomowo

The 3rd Person in Marriage series… THE CHOOSING

[Maiden Edition]

©2021 pst tomowo

ISBN: 9798729047765

The Church in the Air publications.

1192 Rising Moon Trail,

Snellville, GA, 30078, USA

Website: www.air.church

Email: info@air.church

Library of Congress Control Number:

2021902118

Publisher's note:

The reader should not regard the recommendations, ideas and lifestyle practices expressed and described in this book as a substitute for the advice of certified medical specialists or other professionals and experts. The application of such expressed therein is at the reader's sole discretion and risk.

UNTO GOD . . .

'Out of the eater came forth meat, and out of the strong came forth sweetness' (Judges 14:14)

"For this reason shall a man leave his father and mother, and cleave to his wife, and they twain shall be one flesh: so then they are no longer twain, but one flesh. What therefore God hath joined together, let not man put asunder."

(Mark 10:7-9)

'And He said, Unto you it is given to know the mysteries of the kingdom of God: but to others in parables; that seeing they might not see, and hearing they might not understand.'

(Luke 8:10)

CONTENTS...

7. ... AND SHE SAID, YES! 136

8. INTRODUCING THE MARITAL MONSTER... 152

9. ...BEING SINGLE 170

10. MANAGING CRISIS OF CHOOSING IN MARRIAGE... 200

MEET PST TOMOWO ... 248

1. OVERVIEW···

THE 3RD PERSON IN MARRIAGE SERIES.

When the Spirit of GOD nudged me to take on this series, I was super reluctant. Who will not, for this was where I failed the most in my life - Marriage (I thought!).

However, *'Out of the eater came forth meat, and out of the strong came forth sweetness' (Judges 14:14).*

Right in the deepest valley of my failure, I encountered the 3rd Person in Marriage, who began to reveal to me, step by step, precept upon precept, line upon line, how and why marriages fail and why marriages can be successful!

This revelation can only be Divine; *'For unto us it is given to know the mysteries of the Kingdom of GOD: but to others in parables' (Luke 8:10).* Spanning from the Understanding of Marriage to its Preparations, the Choosing, the Compatibilities, Multiplications and its Reigning; this book series will show you WHY your

Marriage is working, so you might keep at it, or WHY it is not working, so you might see a customised way out for you. DISCLAIMER: STRICTLY FOR BELIEVERS!

Millions of experts, mentors, and coaches focus on relationships; tons of books are out there. Similarly, we are all involved in Marriage; whether you are married or not, everyone is a product of a relationship between a man and a woman. We all have a reasonable degree of knowledge and information on how marriages work or how we expect them to be run for a successful outcome.

Therefore, we are appealing to you, have an open mind. Maybe say a simple prayer that GOD helps you see more. We pray this book series increases your knowledge for a better life outcome in the Name of [1]YESHUA HAMASHIACH (JESUS CHRIST). Amen.

The 3rd Person in Marriage -THE CHOOSING: focusing on making the right choice for Marriage. This book delves into why you need to discover yourself before choosing. Are there boundaries in choosing? When to and when not to choose; How to engage Divine Helpers in choosing, and She said, Yes! It is also introducing 'The marital monster' and a peep into being single and happy. Finally, we addressed managing the crisis of choosing in Marriage.

pst tomowo

... setting men up with GOD, for a GLORIOUS TURNAROUND!

---

[1] YESHUA HAMASHIACH is the original Hebrew Name translated to JESUS CHRIST

FAITH BOOST.

"Are you ready for this level? If we live in the Spirit, let us also walk in the Spirit.

We live in the Spirit via waiting on GOD in Praise, Word and Spirit.

However, we walk in the Spirit when we are sensitive to the dictate of the Spirit in our daily dealings because GOD can cause a directive to come anytime and anywhere.

Violent faith makes you restful even in adversity what you do not want. Do not watch. What you do not resist has the right to persist.

What you do not confront, you cannot conquer when GOD speaks. Everything and everyone hears. When the light comes from heaven, he puts you in command. You cannot pray off a prophetic agenda. You can only seek an exemption.

There is no safe place anywhere in the world except in CHRIST. Faith is to be received, brooded upon, and when matured, released at the instance of the presence of Anointing. then acted upon immediately afterwards." **(Excerpts from one of the messages of [2]Bishop David Oyedepo of Living Faith Church. WOFBI).**

....

"Check your emotions at the door. Never think with your eyes because Satan will always show you something that you should see to distract you. Believe with your hearts. Never you look at the difficulty. It will cause you to disbelief the power within you. Above

[2] Bishop David Oedepo, President, Living Faith Church. www.faithtabernacle.org.ng

you and beneath you lies the power that is immeasurable and can change the whole world. Your part is not to create. You are to take advantage of what has already been created.

Ministry is a season of responsibility. Faith insists on possessing possessions. Faith will make you owe things. Faith insists on possessing. Faith refuses to let the heathen keep what belongs to you. Faith is not to be treated as an intellectual puzzle. It should be believed. You don't have to prove it.

Have conversations with GOD. He loves to talk. When you know GOD, serving him will be easy. Faith never has to be proven. Faith is to be believed. Faith will work in your heart, even with doubt in your head if you can believe it. That is all that is required of you. All things are possible to him that believes Spiritually, Physically, and Financially.

Emotional outbursts can limit GOD and cause you not to keep His Word. Don't go by your soul. Follow your heart. Do not try to meet your own needs. Believe GOD, do not believe for deficits. Go for 100 folds. 1000 times. " **(Excerpts from one of the messages of [3]Br. Jesse Duplantis. 'Check your emotions at the door')**

---

[3] Jesse Duplantis. www.jdm.org

SOME

FOUNDATIONAL

TRUTH ON

MARRIAGE

2. SOME FOUNDATIONAL TRUTH ON MARRIAGE···

---

[4]SOME FOUNDATIONAL TRUTH ON MARRIAGE.

*T*o understand the flow, you are to have read the first volume of this series, The 3rd Person in Marriage series: THE PREPARATIONS. We recommend this, and we will be reminding ourselves of some of these Fundamental Truth on Marriage in this chapter. This is culled from the first volume of this series. The Preparations!

When the Spirit of GOD nudged me to take on this series, He told me that in-depth insights and secrets lie in the Bible's pages for a successful relationship. When these revelations were unfolded

---

[4] This chapter is culled from The 3rd Person in Marriage: THE PREPARATIONS

unto me, I was amazed, surprised at the depth of riches of GOD's wisdom and knowledge.

'O the depth of the riches both of the wisdom and knowledge of God, how unsearchable are his judgements, and His ways past finding out.' (Romans 11:33, KJV)

Marriage originated from GOD hence is fully understood through GOD. We are GOD's people; we are not of this world. Marriage is not what the world calls it: Lust, diversity, variation, expressions of perversion, anger or rebellion.

The originator has a Manual for Marriage. We will, therefore, be using His Manual: The Scripture, the very familiar stories of the Bible, to gain insights into the keys to a successful marriage.

Like everything created and valued by GOD, the enemy attacks Marriage immensely at every stage of its life cycle: –The understanding stage (wrong perspective and beliefs on Marriage); preparatory stage (wrong upbringing and abused childhood); choosing stage (wrong timing and choice of partners, or lack of partner); fusion stage (incompatibility at different levels); multiplication stage (unfruitfulness physically, socially and spiritually); and reigning stage (lack of living in fulfilment in life).

Today, due to these attacks, there are many diversities and confusions about Marriage; men with many wives, women with many husbands, multiple divorces, single parents, 'baby mamas', co-habiting partners, 'friends with benefits.' All sorts of relationships that one seems not to know the ideal anymore

19

today, as in the circular world so fully reflected in churches and among Gospel ministers.

This book series aims to reveal the 'IDEAL', the standard with which one can easily stage up one's relationship. It will help see how we are succeeding in relationships to keep it up—and seeing how one is falling short and where to make amends. Praying that as we dive into the revealed steps in the marriage cycle, our eyes of understanding are opened to the gains and flaws in our relationships, birth better relationships and Marriage in JESUS name, Amen.

Because Marriage involves different persons from mostly different backgrounds, this book's examples and practices may require commitments, dedications, and lifestyle modifications for its effectiveness. As with God's Word, they are forever settled in heaven. They work if applied in faith under any conditions or circumstances.

Irrespective of your degree of wholeness or brokenness, we pray that the Light of CHRIST shines on every dark and obscure area of your Marriage and birth you a customised MIRACLE in JESUS name, Amen. Let us dig into this . . .

UNDERSTANDING THE ELEMENTS OF MARRIAGE

In this chapter, we will be looking into the first man in Marriage; The first woman in Marriage; The third person in Marriage; The Godly Marriage, the characteristics of the first man and woman, the offence of the woman, and the redeemed woman.

GOD CREATED ADAM AS MALE AND FEMALE.

In the beginning, Adam was created as Male and Female, complete, lacking in nothing.

So God created man in his own image, in the image of God created He him; male and female created He them. (Genesis 1:27 KJV)

This revelation is further confirmed in chapter five:

"This is the book of the generations of Adam. In the day that GOD created man, in the likeness of God made he him; male and female created he them; and blessed them, and called their name Adam, in the day when they were created." (Genesis 5:1-2 KJV)

'And blessed them, and called their name Adam'. Adam was created as male and female. GOD created Adam completely as a male and female, wanting nothing! Think about this.

MAN AND WOMAN ARE DIFFERENT.

After Adam's creation, GOD put him into the garden he had created for his pleasure and charged him to till and tend the garden. In the course of his duty, while taking care and being in charge of all other creatures God created, behold, none of God's other creatures was like Adam; hence Adam became lonely. Lonely, not because He was not complete, he was lonely because there was no other creature precisely like him! And GOD decided to make a companion for Adam.

Why Woman then? For a variety of men. So there is not only one type of man.

The Lord saw that Adam was the only creature in his class, the image of God. Therefore the Lord promised to make a helpmeet for him. To make this need glaring, the Lord brought all other creatures he created to Adam to see what he would call them. Adam named all creatures and discovered none could meet as a companion for him.

"Then the Lord God took the man and put him in the garden of Eden to tend and keep it.' (Genesis 2:15, NKJV).

And the Lord GOD said, *"it is not good that man should be alone; I will make him a helper <u>comparable to him</u>." (Genesis 2:16, NKJV)*

"So Adam gave names to all cattle, to the birds of the Air, and to every beast of the field. But for Adam, <u>there was not found a helper comparable to him</u>.' (Genesis 2:20 NKJV).

Now, the gap was clear! Adam needed a companion. GOD needs to create another like Adam. Interestingly, however, the whole universe's creator did not go the route or creating a separate being for Adam. He took from Adam to make his companion. Why? Because Adam was created completely ab-initio. Hence, it is simply logical that He separated Adam's female part from him to make Eve.

[21]'And the Lord God caused a deep sleep to fall on Adam, and he slept, and he took one of his ribs and closed up the flesh in its place. [22]Then the rib which the Lord God had taken from man he made into a woman, and he brought her to the man." (Genesis 2:20-22, NKJV).

Point worth nothing.

GOD removed Eve from Adam. Therefore, at the appearance of Eve, Adam becomes incomplete; Eve becomes incomplete!

Therefore, Eve is the completion of Adam. If the woman is the completion of the Man, then Man and woman are different!

The woman is the completion of the Man. Pause, ponder and think about this.

THE 3RD PERSON IN MARRIAGE.

Adam will never be complete without Eve, and vice versa. If this is the case, then there is a need for a unifying force that will always join both!

The all-wisdom GOD decided to fuse Himself into the equation. After all, Adam (as Male and Female) was created in His image and likeness. Now that there is a separation, the GOD factor also is to be brought to the fore.

Adam was in the habit of naming all creatures that GOD brought to him, and whatsoever he called them became their names. After a forced sleep, Eve was presented unto Adam as usual; however, Adam saw a different creature for the first time. 'Bone of my bone'.

Moreover, while Adam was presented with his new companion, the woman, initially part of him, Adam saw beyond the woman. Adam also saw the Spirit of Marriage that joined them together!

For this reason, 'A man shall leave his father and mother and cleaved to his wife. And they shall become one.'... he said.

[23] "And Adam said: "This is now _bone of my bones_ and flesh of my flesh; _she shall be called woman because she was taken out of man._" [24]_Therefore a man shall leave his father and mother and be joined to his wife, and they shall become one flesh._ [25]And they were both naked, the man and his wife, and were not ashamed." (Genesis 2:23-25 NKJV)._

How did Adam understand these two mysteries? At that time, Adam was still operating at his highest frequency, at God's order, hence understanding the deep things of GOD.

> **GOD is the 3rd Person in Marriage.**
>
> **The Cleaving Force.**
>
> **The central force of unity.**

Adam knew by intuition that Eve was taken out of him, hence called her woman. He equally knew that there must be a cleaving of man and woman for them to become One Flesh.

GOD is the third person in Marriage. The Cleaving Force. The central force of unity.

This Truth, further revealed across the scriptures as follows:

A Prophet, Malachi, told the mind of GOD concerning this Truth also:

14 "Yet ye say, Wherefore? Because the Lord hath been witness between thee and the wife of thy youth, against whom thou hath dealt treacherously: yet is she thy companion, and the wife of thy covenant. 15And did not He make One? Yet had He the residue of the Spirit. And wherefore one? That he might seek a Godly seed. Therefore take heed to your Spirit, and let none deal treacherously against the wife of his youth." (Malachi 2:14-15, KJV)

GOD is the Spirit of Marriage. The ONE that makes the couple one!

14'Do you know why? Simple. Because GOD was there as a witness when you spoke your marriage vows to your young bride, and now you've broken these vows, broken the faith-bond with your vowed companion, your covenant wife. 15GOD, not you, made Marriage. His Spirit inhabits even the smallest details of Marriage. And what does He want from Marriage? Children of God, that's what. So guard the Spirit of Marriage within you. Don't cheat on your spouse'. (Malachi 2:14-15, MSG).

GOD is the Spirit of Marriage.

The ONE that makes the couple one!

GOD is the Spirit of Marriage. The ONE that makes the couple one!

ONE God, The ONE. The SPIRIT. All these are addressing the 3rd Person in Marriage!

Our Lord Jesus Christ also brought this truth out clearly in two instances when asked questions about Marriage. He made it clear that it is God that joins Man and Woman. He is the 3rd Person in Marriage.

4 "And He answered and said to them, 'Have you not read that He who made them at the beginning made them male and female, ⁵and said, 'For this reason a man shall leave his father and mother and be joined to this wife, and the two shall become one flesh'? ⁶So then, they are no longer two but one flesh. <u>Therefore what God has joined together, let not man separate</u>." (Matthew 19:4-6, NKJV).

On another occasion, He pointed this Truth out again.

5 "And Jesus answered and said to them, 'Because of the hardness of your heart he (Moses) wrote you this precept. ⁶But from the beginning of the creation, God' made them male and female.' ⁷For this reason a man shall leave his father and mother and be joined to his wife, ⁸and the two shall become one flesh;' so then they are no longer two, but one flesh, ⁹<u>therefore what GOD has joined together, let not man separate</u>." (Mark 10:9, NKJV).

Our Lord Jesus Christ made it clear. It is God that joins Man and Woman in a union! He, therefore, admonishes men not to put this asunder because of the free will choice given them.

Finally, still on this Truth, the Spirit of God furthermore revealed this through Apostle Paul as follows:

¹⁴'For this cause I bow my knees unto the Father of our Lord Jesus Christ, ¹⁵<u>Of whom the whole family in heaven and earth is named.</u>' (Ephesians 3:14-15, KJV).

The whole family in heaven and earth got their names from God. Hello somebody. The 3rd Person in Marriage!

The father of our Lord Jesus Christ, of whom the whole family in heaven and on earth is named. The residue of God in all Marriage. The oneness of God in Marriage. The Spirit of Marriage.

AMEN. AMEN. AMEN.

Acknowledging and referencing this Spirit in Marriage is key to your success in Marriage.

Adam spoke of Him when Eve was brought to him. Prophet Malachi revealed Him as the ONE that makes them one. The Spirit of Marriage. Our Lord Jesus Christ made it clear once and for all. 'What God has joined together,' and Apostle Paul revealed Him as the One of whom the whole family in heaven and earth is named! The 3rd Person in Marriage.

THE GODLY MARRIAGE (GOD + MAN + WOMAN)

Marriage is between God, a Man and a Woman. Man and Woman are different; hence The Spirit of Marriage present to join them.

If your eyes of understanding can grasp this, you are made forever.

Without the 3rd Person in Marriage, there can never be a genuine fusion in Marriage. The 3rd Person in Marriage JOINS the two separate and different beings, fuses them to become one flesh.

Therefore, Every Marriage is a MIRACLE!

Man and Woman are different; they can never be the same or connected and compatible without the help of the 3rd Person in Marriage. The Spirit of Marriage. The ONE that makes them one!

THE CHARACTERISTICS OF THE FIRST MAN AND WOMAN IN MARRIAGE.

Let us see what the first man and the first woman in Marriage look like.

THE CHARACTERISTICS OF THE FIRST MAN.

The scriptures revealed some essential characteristics of the man in the first Marriage. These characteristics will help show the mind of God on who is the man in Marriage. The three basic elements of the man in Marriage are as follows:

1. DOMINION AND AUTHORITY.

Dominion and Authority. Wanting to take charge, wanting to be in control is one of the foremost characteristics. Have you wondered where the phrase 'Man ego' comes from?

Although many lost this trait in upbringing, men fight this even in the face of nothingness because it is key to their manhood.

Dominion and Authority is the very first quality God endowed Adam. When God created Adam, He gave him the mandate of Dominion.

'And God blessed them, and God said unto them, Be fruitful, and multiply, and replenish the earth, and subdue it: and have

28

dominion over the fish of the sea, and over the fowl of the air, and over every living thing that moveth upon the earth.' (Genesis 1:28 KJV)

Then, God placed him in the garden to tend and care for it. God gave Adam dominion mandate. God brought all the creatures He created to Adam to name them, and whatever Adam called them remains their name. Dominion mandate!

Wonder why in Marriage, the name of the Man is significant. Here it is. Man's Dominion and authority are expressed with their domain and territory acquisition. Man wants to dominate, acquire, and build a castle and kingdom for himself. This dominion trait is how they are being wired. Once they acquire someone or something, they are looking for other things to catch. You hear them often say: 'my wife', 'my house, 'my car', my family'.

My, My, My... Dominion and Authority!

[15]*'And the Lord God took the man, and put him into the garden of Eden to dress and to keep it.* [19]*And out of the ground the Lord God formed every beast of the field, and every fowl of the Air, and brought them unto Adam to see what he would call them: and whatsoever Adam called every living creature, that was the name thereof.' (Genesis 2:15,19, KJV).*

Dominion and Authority is the very first characteristic of the Man. They have a sphere and domain to dominate and authority to take charge over. When men are denied this trait, it is as if they are stripped naked. Take a second look at the men in your life, and you will smell dominion and authority from a distance!

2. VISION AND DIRECTION.

Secondly, Man is the one with Vision and Direction. Dominion and Authority work hand in hand with Vision and Direction. They produce a singularity of Purpose, understanding the path to take.

God gave Adam instructions on what to do and what not to do in the garden. God gave Adam the Vision and Direction for life. This is the reason why man is unilateral in thinking. Focus!

Man is the one with the Vision, direction. Man has foresight. It is expected that man take the lead in Vision and direction for the union.

[17]*'And the Lord God took the man, and put him into the garden of Eden to dress it and to keep it. [18]And the Lord God commanded the man, saying, Of every tree of the garden thou mayest freely eat. [19]But of the tree of the knowledge of good and evil, thou shall not eat of it: for in the day that thou eatest thereof thou shall surely die.' (Genesis 2:17-19, KJV).*

Adam was the one with the clear-cut instructions (Vision and Direction) for their lives. This task was not repeated with Eve. Because it was expected that Adam relayed the Vision and Direction to his wife, I guess he failed at this, and this lacuna spoke for itself!

Vision/Direction birth singularity of Purpose. This is why man focuses mainly on one thing at a time. 'I want to eat.' however, after food, he moves on to another thing and forgets about food immediately.

This trouble women a great deal. 'I want sex', and while the woman is still brooding afterwards over the pleasure, men are up and off they go. Why????. Vision and Direction. Focusing on a goal per time.

It is the reason boredom is a significant weakness or issue with men. No matter how good or bad the stuff may be, they are done once they have acquired it. 'What is the next thing on the agenda'. They will say. Repeating the same things over and over can be seen as boredom or nagging to them. Understanding this trait will help a great deal in dealing with this unique species of GOD. Man!

3. STABILITY.

The third essential characteristic of the first Man is Stability. Physical strength. Roughness.Toughness. No hormonal changes. No monthly cycle. Stability! Men are just there. Stable. Ever ready.

Why this Stability, to sustain the weaker vessel made not as stable. Men are wired to be stable. Not for selfish display, it is to support every other thing that is not as stable. This characteristic is evident in men today. As a woman, I wonder why men are so rough, big, strong, and with no hormonal mood swings. They are to bring Stability to the union.

It is a wrong assumption to think or believe that men and women are equal and the same. Irrespective of civilisation, education and socialisation exposures, **men and women are different. However,** men and women deserve an equal right to health, education, wealth, and all the good of life.

Today, this Stability is used as a tool to oppress women in many settings. The same trait meant to protect is used to abuse women.; these things ought not to be so!

There may be more characteristics of the man; however, these three traits form the bedrock upon which every other feature and quality is built. Dominion and Authority. Vision and Direction. Stability. What a BLESSING to see these expressed in the world today!

> *Men and women are different; however, men and women deserve an equal right to health, education, wealth, and all the good of life.*

THE CHARACTERISTICS OF THE FIRST WOMAN.

As with the Man, God did not leave the woman empty. God endowed the woman with her traits. The first woman, Eve, possessed these qualities. These characteristics were fully expressed in Genesis chapters two and three. As Eve expressed herself in Genesis chapter three, her traits and qualities were revealed. What are these qualities?

1. SMARTNESS AND INTUITION.

Smartness is the very first quality of the first woman in Marriage.

32

Remember, God says she is a HELP MEET. That means a Solution Hub. This Smartness can also be called Instinct or Intuition.

"And the Lord GOD said, it is not good that the man should be alone; I will make <u>him an help meet for him</u>.' (Genesis 2:18, NKJV).

A HELPMEET, A Solution Hub, can be liked to today's search engine such as Google. Once you type in something into the Solution Hub, it or she browses around and give you all possible outcomes to the request.

This is the very first trait of the woman. SMARTNESS. A HELPMEET. A SOLUTION HUB. think about this.

Have you wondered where in the world women get their wisdom from? Men and women, exposed to the same thing, and the woman will see more profound things about the stuff. Smartness, it is! One of the traits of the woman! So much that this has landed many women into being bullied, abused, and oppressed. "Why does she know so much. let us stop her!"

To buttress this point, Let us look at how Eve acted by the forbidden Tree. The Bible says both Eve and Adam were standing by the Tree. This action was the main mistake. Remember GOD gave Adam the Vision and Direction. 'Dress and keep the Garden'. However, Adam was not at his duty post.

Unfortunately, Eve, a solution hub, a HELP MEET, will always proffer help and solution everywhere and anywhere she is found. And since they were both standing by the forbidden tree. Eve went to work. And the enemy took advantage of her smartness

33

to beguile her. She browsed the tree and saw three reasons why she must eat of it as against one reason God gave Adam not to!

Let us see the rendition below:

'And when the woman saw that the tree was good for food, and that it was pleasant to the eyes, and a tree to be desired to make one wise, she took of the fruit thereof, and did eat, and gave also unto her husband with her, and he did eat.' (Genesis 3:6, KJV).

The Devil, through the serpent, did not tell her those. She saw them by herself. She browsed the tree profoundly and saw many reasons to eat it versus the only reason God gave Adam!

Instinct. Smartness. Insight into things. Multi-dimensional. She brought help to the wrong place! Do you see this in women today? Eve was not adequately informed of the Vision; secondly, Adam was not at his duty post, hence exposing all of Eve's smartness to the wrong thing and wrong place!

The enemy told Eve of one reason to eat the fruit. Eve saw three reasons why she could not miss eating the fruit. Smartness. Instinct. The intuition of a woman is unparalleled. Any man that tries to compete with a woman does that at his peril.

Today, many men stoop so low to get very small, young and uneducated girls to marry, and to their surprise, in a few years, those unexposed girls are in control!

Smartness. The intuition of a woman. My advice, do not compete with a woman!. (Just a joke)

2. INFLUENCE.

As seen in the first woman's life, Eve, the very second trait of a woman is INFLUENCE. Though women are not endowed to lead, dominate or have directions. However, women are highly equipped for Influence. Women influence Authority. Women influence Leaders, Women influence Dominion. Women influence Visions. Women influence Strongmen. Think about this!

"And when the woman saw that the tree was good for food, and that it was pleasant to the eyes, and a tree to be desired to make one wise, <u>she took of the fruit thereof, and did eat, and gave also unto her husband with her; and he did eat</u>." (Genesis 3:6, KJV)

Eve did not only eat the fruit, she also gave the fruit to her husband with her, and he ate it!

"Behold, thy people in the midst of thee are women: the gates of thy land shall be set wide open unto thine enemies: the fire shall devour thy bars." (Nahum 3:13 KJV)

Although natural women are not given Vision and Direction, nor can they lead effectively, what is home with women is the ability to influence Authority. Because of her multi-dimensional approach to things, a woman will see all the possible ways to influence Authority.

Delilah asked Samson of the secret to his power three times, she used it against him three times, yet Samson kept revealing it to her until she brought doom to him! (Judges 16)

The woman's influential ability is because of her multi-dimensional way of reasoning. The woman will see things in so many ways and try all the many ways until she gets her way!

The influence of a woman is unparalleled —a solution hub. Saddled with several ways to achieve things, one out of her million ways will hit the target!

Hmmmmmmmmm...

3. BEAUTY.

Beauty is another characteristic of the first woman. Adam was captivated by his woman. Having seen and named several creatures, when Adam saw Eve, he went all the way for her! She is 'the bone of my bones, flesh of my flesh.'

Have you wondered why women are so pretty, shapely, soft–talking, sweet voice, smooth face, fantastic smile, waist twisting, slim arms? Think about that! BEAUTY is a trait endowed every woman!

[22]And the rib, which the Lord God had taken from man, made he a woman, and brought her unto the man. [23]and Adam said: "This is now <u>bone of my bones</u> *and flesh of my flesh;* <u>she shall be called woman</u> *because she was taken out of man." (Genesis 2:22-23, NKJV).*

Forever, man will always have eyes for the beauty of the woman. It is evident in our world today. So much that women's beauty is being used as a tool for all manner of goals, such as for advertisement, influence, setting traps for great men. etc.

The woman's three characteristics: Smartness, Influence, and Beauty, were not made in error by GOD. The woman was made with good intention.

However, the woman's offence caused so much havoc to creation that if this was not addressed, one might not appreciate the actual purpose of the woman's traits. I have heard from many quarters that women are the source of trouble in the world. Hmmmmmm. Maybe not. Let us take a look into this.

THE OFFENSE OF THE WOMAN . . .

The multi-dimensional ways of seeing things and reasoning drive women not to stick to one direction or authority. This approach may come up as no reference for Vision and order because vision and focus were not dittoed her. Hence, a need for natural women to be under the guidance of some sort always!

Women naturally present as lawbreakers. They enjoy breaking the rules, and their makeup gives them multiple options. When not guided, they will explore these options even at the expense of breaking God's law and instructions.

This offence was what happened in the Garden of Eden. Eve could not adhere to a single law without Adam's support and insistence on Vision and Direction. Applying the Smartness, Intuition and Influence on wrong things and inappropriate places is the 'Offense of the Woman.'

This offence has led many women to usurp authority instead of influencing it. As a helpmeet, a solution hub, care must be taken to guide a natural woman in the right direction, or else, she will become a solution for evil deeds!

Therefore, a woman with no vision, direction and external support may severely derail, leading to pain and destruction.

> **This is the Offense of the Woman: Applying the Smartness, Intuition and Influence on wrong things and in inappropriate places.**

According to the scriptures: the single lady must be under her father and a married lady under her husband's guidance. She can be easily deceived when not guided.' Satan tempted and deceived Eve, not Adam' says the scriptures. (1 Timothy 2:14) However, Eve influenced Adam.

This approach still happens today. Delilah and Samson. She pressed on him several times, yet, Samson fell all the time!

Because of the woman's nature, a multi-dimensional rationing being, if she is not helped and supported with vision and directions (a trait she does not possess naturally), she can be susceptible to distractions and instability. According to the custom of Israelites, women were to be in guidance of a sort, always. *(Numbers 30:5-8, KJV)*

In today's world, we promote women's freedom from oppression, bullying, domestic and societal violence, and gender inequality (which is okay and very important, by the way). Sometimes, however, this gender equality goes to the extreme, where women become unaccountable to anyone.

This unaided liberty is a dangerous state to be in if there is no external guiding support of some sort for her.

An ungodly woman is the most dangerous tool a man can have. Satan knows this, and he uses such women extensively for evil deeds today.

> **A Godly woman is the most precious tool that any man can possess.**

A free-spirited woman is a dangerous tool in the hands of the evil ones!

"As a Jewel of gold in a swine's snout, so is a fair woman which is without discretion." (Proverbs 11:22, KJV)

Moreover, as a woman's brain functions multi-dimensionally, so is her mouth; hence, talkativeness is a prevalent weakness of women.

No wonder the scriptures urge women to be in silence in Church. (Not the Spirit-controlled women, of course!)

God suffers not a woman to preach. A natural woman. A non-Spirit-controlled woman cannot handle the things of God right! They are instead to learn in silence.

"Let a woman learn in silence with all submission." (1 Timothy 2:11, NKJV)

THE WOMAN AT REDEMPTION.

At redemption, this offence is done with. All the curses that go with this offence had been redeemed by the Blood of our Lord Jesus Christ.

The Bible says we are redeemed by the Blood of our Lord Jesus Christ, including the sins of the first woman's offence.

'In whom we have redemption through His Blood, even the forgiveness of sins.' (Colossians 1:14, NKJV).

Therefore, as many as are led by the Spirit of God; these are the sons of God. For in CHRIST. No male, no female, no Jew, no gentile, no bond, no free.

"There is therefore now no condemnation to them which are in CHRIST JESUS, who walk not after the flesh, but after the Spirit." (Romans 8:1, KJV)

[27]'For as many of you as were baptised into Christ have put on Christ. [28]There is neither Jew nor Greek, there is neither slave nor free, there is neither male nor female; for you are all one in Christ Jesus. [29]And if you are Christ's, then you are Abraham's seed, and heirs according to the promise.' (Galatians 3:27-29 NKJV)

When a natural woman receives our Lord Jesus Christ as her Lord and Saviour and submits to the Holy Spirit's Lordship, She becomes guided and influenced by the Holy Spirit that now lives inside of her. Hence, submitting to other authorities becomes easy.

'For as many as are led by the Spirit of God, these are sons of God.' (Romans 8:14 NKJV)

A Godly woman is the most precious tool that any man can possess!

'He who finds a wife finds a good thing, and obtains favour from the Lord.' (Proverbs 18:22 NKJV)

The woman is the 'PRAY-ER' of her husband and household. When a woman makes praying for her husband her sole responsibility, she gives birth to a great man.

You do not need to know how to pray as a woman. The ability to pray is inherent in every woman. If she can be silent in prayers, her prayers will make the man and her family!

Instead of talking and discussing all in her mind, If she can be quiet and allow all the smartness in her converged into prayers, she will make great men on earth. Most of her discussion would be sorted in prayers!

As a Life Coach, the Spirit of GOD taught us how to 'Gossip with JESUS' in our coaching program. Just tell JESUS. Just let Him know about it all. This practice is so homely and natural with women. Many outstanding miracles have been born through this!

Think about this. 'Gossip with JESUS?' When a woman submits in silence, in prayers. Then God uses her to perfect the man. And the man becomes his best. 'It is not good for a man to be alone. I will, therefore, make him a helpmeet for him.' (Genesis 2:18).

The woman is the helpmeet for man; to equip the man to fulfil the mandate of God's Blessing on the earth: To be fruitful, multiply, replenish the earth, subdue it and have Dominion. That is why the Bible says:

'He who finds a wife finds a good thing and obtains favor from the Lord.' (Proverbs 18:22 NKJV)

THE GODLY MARRIAGE. (GOD + MAN + WOMAN)

The Godly Marriage is the combination of a man, a woman and God in action! The Man to bring to fore; Dominion / Authority; Vision /Direction; and Stability. The Woman presenting Insights/ Smartness; Influence; and Beauty. The Spirit of Marriage strengthening man and empowering woman. What a combination!

No man can exhibit all of these traits without the help of the Spirit of God. So also, no woman can ever effectively use her smartness positively without her submission to the Spirit of God! The Spirit of oneness, God, making a man with foresight and enabling the woman with insight! This is the Godly Marriage. There is no error in God!

This chapter is an abridged excerpt on the foundational Truth of Marriage. The detailed explanations and scriptural expositions to this chapter are addressed in the first volume of this series. The 3rd Person In Marriage: THE PREPARATIONS. I hope you avail yourself of this volume since reading the book will help to understand better our conversation on this series.

THE PREPARATIONS FOR MARRIAGE.

The Preparations of The 3rd Person in Marriage Series, focusing mainly on the preparatory stage in Marriage and targeting how and why the need for preparation and the specific preparations needed for a successful marital relationship.

What we see today as the crisis in marriages are not born only from the immediate two or so years of Marriage. They are deep-seated in our upbringings—the very core of our makeup. Many of the difficulties and incompatibilities in relationships are because of ill- upbringing. The Spirit of GOD began to nudge me as He exposed to me the need to prepare for Marriage when we were young; otherwise, future failures will be inevitable.

Even if this preparatory stage exposes many flaws in your characters, the intention is to help reveal the reasons behind the raw materials you brought into your Marriage, hence seeing how and why your Marriage is working or not working.

As encouraged earlier, have an open mind, let the Holy Spirit show you an X-ray of your personality and that of your spouse, so you might see what and what to continue with and what to improve upon or be done away with. in your relationship.

We will be looking into the need and why Preparing the boy for Marriage; Preparing the girl for Marriage; Raising a Godly man; Raising a Godly woman; Who actually am I? Engaging 'the 3rd person in marriage' in Preparations; and Managing crisis due to faulty preparations for Marriage.

Having been saddled with the basic understanding of Marriage, let us now move to the very next step, looking into the nitty-gritty of why and what to prepare for in Marriage. *(see details in The 3rd Person in Marriage: THE PREPARATIONS).*

....

THE CHOOSING in Marriage is the core of this volume: After a seasoned foundation and preparations for Marriage, the choice you make is the next crucial step to a successful marriage outcome. Why the right choice for Marriage? How and when to choose, any boundaries in choosing, engaging Divine helpers, and being single and happy, among others. Let us dig into this...

Your Notes . . .

Understanding some foundational truth of Marriage. Adam was created as male and female; Man and woman are different, the first man and woman's characteristics. The 3rd Person in Marriage, and the Godly Marriage between God, man and woman. How did you see these truths today? Please explain.

The 3rd Person in

DISCOVER YOU

BEFORE

CHOOSING

3. DISCOVER YOU BEFORE CHOOSING···

DISCOVER YOU BEFORE CHOOSING.

WHO ARE YOU?

Who are you? Do you know, what is unique about you, why you? Who are you? Let us see some examples here and pay attention to how these persons are described in the Bible.

JACOB AND ESAU.

²⁴'So when her days were fulfilled for her to give birth, indeed there were twins in her womb. ²⁵And the first came out red. He was like a hairy garment all over; so they called his name Esau. ²⁶Afterwards, his brother came out, and his hand took hold of Esau's heel; so his name was called Jacob. Isaac was sixty years old when she bore them. ²⁷So the boys grew. And Esau was a skillful

48

hunter, a man of the field; but Jacob was a mild man, dwelling in tents. 28And Isaac loved Esau because he ate of his game, but Rebekah loved Jacob." (Genesis 25:24-28 NKJV)

JEREMIAH.

"Before I formed you in the womb I knew you; before you were born I sanctified you; I ordained you a prophet to the nations." (Jeremiah 1:5 NKJV)

JOHN THE BAPTIST.

13"But the angel said to him, "do not be afraid, Zacharias, for your prayer is heard; and your wife Elizabeth will bear you a son, and you shall call his name John. 14And you will have joy and gladness, and many will rejoice at his birth.

16And he will turn many of the children of Israel to the Lord their GOD." (Luke 1:13-14, 16 NKJV)

JESUS CHRIST.

30"Then the angel said to her, "do not be afraid, Mary, for you have found favor with GOD. 31And behold, you will conceive in your womb and bring forth a son, and shall call his name JESUS. 32He will be great, and will be called the son of the Highest; and the Lord GOD will give him the throne of his father David. 33And he will reign over the house of Jacob forever, and of his kingdom there will be no end." (Luke 1:30-33 NKJV)

WHO ARE YOU? REALLY

You are somebody. You are unique. You are an essential personality, and you are God's BEST. Irrespective of what your family calls you, community, or the world tag you, there is something extraordinary about you. You have to discover yourself to enjoy the fullness of life. Many today live based on the idea of who they think they are; many live based on what others call them and live a short-changed life.

In the context of Choosing in Marriage, many choose their life partners before discovering who they are. When they finally found themselves, they realised that the selected partner did not fit their actual status.

WHEN NOT TO CHOOSE A PARTNER.

In choosing a life partner in marriage, there are times when it is not advisable to make such a decision. Such times are when in a crisis, in deliverance prayer meetings, in breakthrough class, in trying times, when at a low state, when in a quest for who you are, when broken and battered, when recently promoted, when recently got a job or business.

These times, you do not know the fullness of who you are. The present circumstances could mask your true identity, hence a wrong time to choose for Marriage. You are not in your rested state, either low or overjoyed. Many irrational decisions can be made at these times. These times are a season of one's life, the season will eventually pass, and more apparent realities will be dawn. These times are to be avoided as much as possible. Marriage is not for a season; Marriage is for all seasons of life.

Maturity comes faster for some and slower for others. Therefore, one cannot and should not base maturity solely only on age. Due to family background, exposure, and life circumstances, many take up responsibilities earlier than others. As much as age is still a factor, discovering who you are is the key to maturity. Therefore, let us address the point of discussion; who are you?

WHO ARE YOU?

Discovering who you are may not necessarily be by finding the fullness or a full-blown discovery of oneself. It may not be the fullness of someone's manifestation. It may simply be a seed, a picture, a clear idea, a fragment of what and who you are! However, a glimpse of knowing who you are is needed before deciding on a life partner.

The complete discovery can be built upon with time; hence discovering who you are is not waiting until you are in the full stature of it. Not until you made all the money, achieved all goals, or attained the pinnacle of your career or business.

Discovering who you are is understanding the route and direction for your life!

BASIC HUMAN DISCOVERY OF WHO YOU ARE.

For centuries now, the human behavioural patterns are broadly grouped into introverts and extroverts; these are further grouped into four temperaments: The Melancholic, Phlegmatic, Sanguine and Choleric temperaments.

In his book 'Spirit-controlled temperament,' [5]Tim Lahaye dealt extensively with these four temperaments and how we can allow the Spirit of God to manage and control these traits for a better life outcome. I recommend this book to all.

Because of the importance and relevance of the different traits and temperaments to this topic, 'Discover you before choosing', we shall be looking briefly into them as follows. It is encouraged to see details in the Book described above.

MELANCHOLY -EXTREME INTROVERTS.

These individuals tend to be analytical, detail-oriented, and are deep thinkers and feelers. They are shy persons, and they avoid being singled out in a crowd. A melancholic personality leads to self-reliant individuals who are thoughtful, reserved, and often anxious. They often strive for perfection within themselves and their surroundings, which leads to tidy and detailed-oriented behaviours.

---

[5] Tim LaHaye, Spirit controlled Temperaments.

PHLEGMATIC.

A phlegmatic individual tends to be relaxed, peaceful, quiet, and easy-going. They are sympathetic and care about others, yet try to hide their emotions. Phlegmatic individuals also are good at generalising ideas or problems to the world and making compromises.

SANGUINE.

Sanguine is a personality type expressed as enthusiastic, active, and social. Sanguine individuals tend to be more extroverted and enjoy being part of a crowd; they find that being social, outgoing, and charismatic is easy to accomplish. Individuals with this personality have a hard time doing nothing and engage in more risk-seeking behaviour.

CHOLERIC -EXTREME EXTROVERTS.

Choleric individuals also tend to be more extroverted. They are described as being independent, decisive, and goal-oriented. They enjoy being in charge of a group since they have many leadership qualities as well as ambition. Choleric personalities also have a logical and fact-based outlook on the world.

SPIRIT-CONTROLLED YOU: THE UNIQUE YOU

Everyone falls into these four described temperaments above, manifesting their expressed traits, strengths and weakness. We are more aligned to this set of temperaments than to our colour or racial differences.

As believers, there is another set of people, these as Tim LaHaye called them; 'The Spirit Controlled Temperament.' Having received Jesus Christ as their Lord and Saviour and now filled with the Holy Ghost, these people allow the Spirit of God to boost their inherent strengths and minimise their weaknesses.

They produce a unique Melancholic, Spirit-controlled Melancholic, a Spirit-controlled Phlegmatic, a Spirit-controlled Sanguine and Spirit-controlled Choleric traits. **This uniqueness is you with the influence of the Spirit of God. This new you stand you out!**

In discovering yourself before choosing in Marriage; It is crucial first to identify where you belong in the four different major temperaments. Some exhibit a combination of the traits, identify where you belong, and study these groups' strengths and weaknesses; It will interest you to see that many of the ways you behave align with the temperaments class you belong to.

This classification is the fundamental level of discovering you. Please, it is highly advisable to make this discovery as early as possible, especially in teenage years and highly recommended for teenagers in your care. It sure helps to understand oneself more and reduce the floods of identity confusion in the world today.

Therefore, who are you? A Melancholic, Phlegmatic, Sanguine, Choleric, or a combination of two different temperaments. What are the strengths and weaknesses associated with these temperaments or types of combinations?

How many of these strengths and weaknesses are you currently exhibiting in your life? Please pay attention to them as they form a basic understanding of who you are.

When you allow the Holy Spirit to dwell and operate in and through you, a new personality is formed; this is the Spirit-Controlled You.

This is the unique you!

After we have identified and understood the basic traits you possess, it is now time to go further to discover who you are in CHRIST.

Despite your basic personality, **when you allow the Holy Spirit to dwell and operate in and through you, a new personality is formed; this is the Spirit-Controlled You.**

This is the unique you, the best you, and the You that stands out in the crowd, even among similar temperaments and personalities class.

This unique you is what is needed to prosper in life. Let us see some examples from the Bible.

Biblical Examples of Spirit Controlled Personalities.

I. Jacob vs Israel.

Jacob, the second son of Isaac, was known for his supplanting, dubious and trickster character until he encountered God and his life changed; his name also changed into Israel.

27'So He said to him, "What is your name?" He said, "Jacob." 28And He said, "Your name shall no longer be called Jacob, but Israel; for you have struggled with God and with men, and have prevailed." 29Then Jacob asked, saying, "Tell me Your name, I pray." And He said, "Why is it that you ask about My name?" And He blessed him there. 30So Jacob called the name of the place Peniel: For I have seen God face to face, and my life is preserved." (Genesis 32:27-30 NKJV)

II. Simon vs Simon Peter.

Our Lord Jesus Christ surnamed Simon, the son of Jonah, Peter. This event happened when Simon encountered the Anointing, CHRIST, The Messiah, revealed to him by God the Father; this encounter earned Simon a key to the gates of Heaven, upon which the Church is built.

13"when Jesus came into the region of Caesarea Philippi, he asked his disciples, saying, 14 "Who do men say that I, the son of man, am?" So they said, "some say John the Baptist, some Elijah, and others Jeremiah or one of the prophets." [15]He said to them, "but who do you say that I am?" [16]Simon Peter answered and said, "You are the CHRIST, the son of the living God."

[17]Jesus answered and said to him, "Blessed are you, Simon bar-Jonah, for flesh and blood has not revealed this to you, but my father who is in heaven. [18]And I also say to you that you are Peter, and on this rock I will build my Church, and the gates of hades shall not prevail against it.

[19]And I will give you the keys of the kingdom of heaven, and whatever you bind on earth will be bound in heaven, and whatever you loose on earth will be loosed in heaven." [20]Then he commanded his disciples that they should tell no one that he was Jesus the CHRIST." (Matthew 16:13-20 NKJV)

III. Saul vs Paul.

Saul, a devoted Pharisee and lawyer of the tradition of Jew, was going about silencing the Christians he taught were opposing the laid down traditions of the Jews until he met with Jesus Christ Himself. His life was transformed, his name changed, and he became the crusader of faith in Christ, the same purpose he was attacking earlier!

[3]'As he journeyed he came near Damascus, and suddenly a light shone around him from heaven. [4]Then he fell to the ground, and heard a voice saying to him, "Saul, Saul, why are you persecuting Me?" [5]And he said, "Who are You Lord?" Then the Lord said, "I am

Jesus, whom you are persecuting, it is hard for you to kick against the goods." ⁶So he, trembling and astonished, said, "Lord, what do You want me to do?" Then the Lord said to him, "Arise and go into the city, and you will be told what you must do."

⁷And the men who journeyed with him stood speechless, hearing a voice but seeing no one. ⁸Then Saul arose from the ground, and when his eyes were opened he saw no one. But they led him by the hand and brought him into Damascus. ⁹And he was three days without sight, and neither ate nor drank.' (Acts 9:3-9 NKJV)

Do not stop at being a melancholic, phlegmatic, sanguine, or choleric personality; be a Spirit-controlled you.

Be a mixture of the Spirit of GOD plus you. That is who GOD fashions you to be, for you are fearfully and wonderfully made!

As a believer, you may not experience a very striking and miraculous point of contact with GOD like the above examples.

However, everyone who gives their life to Jesus Christ and allows the Holy Spirit to dwell and operate through them; equally has a transformed life similar to those listed above! The Same Spirit, delivering men from the rule and dominion of darkness and translating them into the kingdom of Jesus Christ. It is a transformed life. Even if there is no striking manifested encounter to this effect, this is still a changed life.

13'He has delivered us from the power of darkness and conveyed us into the kingdom of the Son of His love, 14in whom we have redemption through His blood, the forgiveness of sins.' (Colossians 1:13-14 NKJV)

Do not stop at being a melancholic, phlegmatic, sanguine, or choleric personality; be a Spirit-controlled you. Be a mixture of the Spirit of God plus you. That is who God fashions you to be, for you are fearfully and wonderfully made.

"I will praise you, for I am fearfully and wonderfully made; marvellous are your works, and that my soul knows very well." (Psalms 139:14 NKJV)

HOW DO YOU DISCOVER WHO YOU ARE?

The best way to understand the equipment is to study its manufacturer's manual. To discover who you are, you have to ask from your manufacturer; GOD, your creator; what He says about you is what you are.

Let us see some examples here:

Our saviour Jesus Christ accepted the volume of what was written about Him. He aligned with them, hence fulfilling destiny. He said, today, this scripture is fulfilled in your eyes.

"Then I said, 'Behold, I have come— in the volume of the book it is written of Me— To do Your will, O God.' (Hebrews 10:7 NKJV)

As mentioned earlier, Simon Peter earned his own identity as Peter, A rock! upon discovering who CHRIST is.

When you discover JESUS CHRIST, you will find your authentic you!

Apostle Paul, whose name changed from Saul to Paul upon encounter with Our Lord Jesus Christ, revealed a treasure that believers must encounter in their faith journey in Christ. He emphasised that the encounter with Christ is and can only be by revelation, and he earnestly prayed that all believers in Ephesus encounter this revelation.

> *When you discover JESUS CHRIST, you will find your authentic you!*

IT IS BY REVELATION TO DISCOVER JESUS CHRIST...

Paul prayed that every believer needs this prayer; upon salvation, this prayer is essential to encounter and discover you in Christ.

[15]"Therefore I also, after I heard of your faith in the Lord Jesus and your love for all the saints, [16]not cease to give thanks for you, making mention of you in my prayers: [17]that the God of our Lord Jesus Christ, the father of glory, may give to you the Spirit of

wisdom and revelation in the knowledge of him, [18]the eyes of your understanding being enlightened; that you may know what is the hope of his calling, what are the riches of the glory of his inheritance in the saints, [19]and what is the exceeding greatness of his power toward us who believe, according to the working of his mighty power" (Ephesians 1:15-19 NKJV).

If you do not know who Christ is, you will not know who you are! Your 'spiritually and CHRIST revealed you' is superior to the forces of darkness and is the prop for authentic success in life.

Many today are living on half-truth of who they are. Many go through life without discovering their true identity. Many take solace in aligning with their profession, gifting, and vocation as who they are; some even rely on what people say about them to be who they are; little wonder there is a flood of identity confusion in the world today.

The good news is there is a way out. As you discover who CHRIST is, you will discover your identity. When this is done, you will be very contented, satisfied and you will fulfil destiny. How then can one discover Christ in very practical terms? Let us get into it.

SOME STEPS ON HOW TO DISCOVER YOU IN CHRIST.
I. Engage the 'Almighty formula.'

Our ministry runs an online coaching programme called LIFE Coaching; it is an online retreat where we set men up with GOD for a GLORIOUS TURNAROUND. A flexible, self-paced, need-specific, mobile-friendly online retreat. One of the practices we engage in is creating an atmosphere for God's Glory. This practice is what we call *'The Almighty Formula.'*

The Almighty Formula is engaging 30 minutes High Praise + 30 minutes Waiting on the Word + 30 minutes Mingling with the Holy Ghost, Every day.

As one engages this simply practice, you will become more aligned with God and His ways, hence discovering who you are in Christ, your unique competitive advantage for success in life. You may want to consider this. Many engaging this practice comes with catalogues of testimonies; we pray you to have yours too. We will like to hear from you about your experiences engaging the 'Almighty Formula'. Some more details about our LIFE Coaching is here www.coaching.air.church You can also email us at info@air.church

II. Pray the Pauline prayers.

Apostle Paul prayed that all Christians encounter the revelational knowledge of our Lord JESUS CHRIST according to Ephesians 1: 15-19. My father in the Lord, [6]Br. Kenneth E. Hagin said in his books and messages that he set out to pray these Pauline prayers (Ephesians 1:17-23, and Ephesians 3:14-21) for many months,

---

[6] Kenneth E. Hagin. www.rhema.org

focusing on these scriptures every day in prayers and waiting on them. After about eight months, he sure was granted revelational encounters with our Lord Jesus Christ. Many of such Blessing from these encounters are a BLESSING to the Church today.

How do you engage the Pauling prayers, just read them, pray them, focusing and wait on them for an encounter. When you spend time on such scriptures, revelational insights are granted to you. The Bible says that:

'Blessed are those who hunger and thirst for righteousness, for they shall be filled'. (Matthew 5:6, NKJV).

One day, the Spirit of GOD told me that ***'The Word of GOD is not just the Bible, the Word of GOD is HIDDEN inside the Bible, you have to dig deep to encounter Him.'***

When you spend enough time, long enough to wait on the Word of GOD, you will encounter the Word of LIFE, which will turn things around for you as you discover your New You. Your Unique You. Your 'You in CHRIST'!

III. Raise an altar of Vision.

As you engage the Almighty Formula, engaging the Pauline Prayers, and fellowshipping with the Almighty GOD, revelations, insights and understandings of the scriptures and how they relate to you will be dropped into your Spirit.

Write these down; more understanding of visions and directions for life will be trickled down into your heart. Embrace them, write them down, and begin to engage them, taking appropriate actions required. This practice is what we call 'Raising and Altar of Vision'. The insights and revelations granted you in the place of fellowship with GOD have a great capacity to birth success and breakthroughs in you. This practice reveals your unique you.

IV. Let CHRIST be formed in you.

Give attention to fellowshipping with GOD, engaging the presence of GOD, and then making an effort to practice the Word of GOD you are engaging. It is in the practice of the Word of GOD that the transformation of life occurs. When you read and engage a scripture, go a step further and practice it. Take the corresponding actions. Behave as the Word talks about, and let your life reflects the Word of GOD. Insist on becoming what the Word of God says about you.

For example, the Bible says:

'And God blessed them, and God said to them, 'Be fruitful and Multiply; fill the earth and subdue it, have dominion over the fish of the sea, over the birds of the air, and over every living thing that moves on the earth.' (Genesis 1:28 NKJV)

Receive this scripture; it is your dominion mandate. Speak it forth over your life every day, expects its manifestations in your life.

Look out for them as you set out in your vocation, career, studies or business. Expect fruitfulness, expect multiplications, and expect your business to be popular, filling the earth, expect your skills to be on high demands everywhere. Expect your abilities to subdue every opposition on your way. Expect to reign in Dominion to the Glory of GOD! This way, you are allowing CHRIST to form in you.

All scriptures have the capacity to become what they say.

'Who Himself bore our sins in His own body on the tree, that we, having died to sins, might live for righteousness- by whose stripes you were healed.' (1 Peter 2:24 NKJV). Expect divine healing for all sickness, Insist, and you will live in Divine sound health.

'And God is able to make all grace abound toward you, that you, always having all sufficiency in all things, may have an abundance for every good work.' (2 Corinthians 9:8 NKJV)

Expect to have all needs met. Believe that in you is everything you need and will attract everything you need for success in life, career, business, vocations, and ministry because *'GOD is making all grace abound towards you.'* And as you engage the Word of GOD in this way, insisting on the Word, they will become your realities. This practice is how to let CHRIST form in you.

Such a one that lives a life in CHRIST this way allowing CHRIST formed in him or her, such a one becomes a unique man or woman, a unique boy or girl; such a one will stand out in the crowd. Such a one will know no shame; they will step into the BLESSING of GOD and become a joy to many generations.

Such a man is qualified and is ready to decide who should be his life partner. Discovering yourself helps you see clearly, who you would like to have beside you all your life. As you embark on finding yourself, your status will change; you will no longer be comfortable with some people's characters and attributes.

Your status will change. New friends are brought into your circle. Deciding at this new stage will be among your mate, like-minded, BLESSING provoking, CHRIST Kingdom-minded people. This way, your connectivity will be beyond mere physical or temperament connectivity.

V. Building your Characteristics as a Man or Woman

From the above chapter, especially in the first volume of this series:' The 3rd Person in Marriage', we dealt extensively with the first man and first woman's basic characteristics. These traits are what the manual expect of all desiring to be in the marriage relationship.

As you desire to choose Marriage, you must discover where you are on the radar. Do you have the traits of a man? Authority/dominion, vision/direction, and stability? Are you a Godly man? Do you have the characteristics of a woman?

Smartness/instinct, influence, and beauty? Are you a Godly woman?

Before deciding who to marry, this is an excellent time to build up your basic characteristics as a man or a woman. Irrespective of your background, you can begin to identify any lack in your characteristics and work on making you a better man or woman for your future life partner. Even if you have an angel as a life partner, the union will still be flawed if you do not contribute your traits to the relationship.

Hence, in discovering you before choosing, this is the time to read that book 'The 3rd Person in Marriage. THE PREPARATIONS'. Take all the exercises, identify how your background has influenced your characteristics, as a man or a woman, seek redress for major background and preparations deficits with the help of the 3rd Person in Marriage, The God Almighty, and build yourself up in the areas you are lacking.

This point leads to the conclusion of discovering yourself before deciding on Marriage. A quick recap: Go for the basic discovering of yourself by aligning with the general four temperaments, Melancholic, Phlegmatic, Sanguine, and Choleric. See where you fall, the strengths and the weaknesses.

Then go a step further to discover yourself in CHRIST, which is your competitive advantage. Engage the Almighty Formula for the presence of GOD, Pray the Pauline prayers, Raise an altar of

Vision, and Let CHRIST be formed in you as you practice the Word of GOD and live them out. Finally, build your characteristics as a man and a woman using the characteristics of the first man, Adam, and the first woman, Eve, as a standard. Become a Godly man or woman.

Doing the above will be the most significant investment you will and could ever engage in your life. The dividends from these discoveries will birth success not only in your Marriage, even beyond; you will also invoke God's BLESSING in every area of your life. By the way, these investments are not cumbersome in any way; they are lifestyle modifications; they will add to you, regardless of your race, colour, economic status, geographical location, education, or skill inclinations.

After an excellent job on the above, now, it is time to seek GOD's face over your life partner; and you can be guaranteed of GOD's speed! Our GOD is good, and His mercies endure forevermore, Amen. In reality, many people did not go through these processes before making that choice for their life partner. Many people are not taught. Many just follow their peer groups or family traditional ways of doing things; well, you are not alone in that club!

Maybe you are already married; let this piece reveal to you some of the gaps and possible reasons for your crisis in Marriage, and together with the help of the 3rd Person in Marriage, make amends. However, if you happen to be reading this piece and are yet to enter into the marriage institution, please endeavour to practice these suggestions; they will only make life easier for you.

As spelt out in the earlier chapter, the practices and references in this book are guides, a standard to align up your relationship. There are many approaches and ways of dealing with life crisis. Are these suggestions and exercises attainable? By all means, YES! However, this will require willing hearts to allow the 3rd Person in Marriage to fix all the gaps as He gives you a customised miracle and way out for your relationship!

Your Notes:

Who are you? Do you know?

What are the steps to take to discover your unique you?

Did you discover yourself before choosing Marriage?

If not, what are the deficits you now see in your Marriage due to this error in choosing? List them out.

Your Notes.

Will you be willing to let the 3rd Person in Marriage work with you and, for you, a customised way out of these problems? Because there is a way out!

How will you engage GOD to step into this area of your Marriage?

The 3rd
Person in
Marriage

THE
BOUNDARIES
IN CHOOSING

4. THE BOUNDARIES IN CHOOSING···

THE BOUNDARIES IN CHOOSING A LIFE PARTNER.

MAN IS A TRIUNE BEING.

*M*an is a Spirit, Man has a soul (the seat of his will, intellect, mind and emotions), and Man lives in a body.

Genesis chapter two verse seven and Hebrews chapter two, verses six to eight, explicitly revealed that man was created with a higher matter than the earth: The breath of GOD. Man can have dominion over the world and everything on the earth.

'And the Lord God formed man of the dust of the ground, and breathed into his nostrils the breathe of life, and man became a living being.' (Genesis 2:7 NKJV)

6'But one testified in a certain place, saying: "What is man that You are mindful of him, or the son of man that You take care of him? 7You have made him a little lower than the angels; You have crowned him with glory and honor, and set him over the works of Your hands. 8You have put all things in subjection under his feet." For in that He put all in subjection under him, He left nothing that is not put under him. But now we do not yet see all things put under him.' (Hebrews 2: 6-8 NKJV)

Man is created with a higher matter than the earth; hence, man can easily dominate everything. Man is a Spirit, has a Soul (the seat of your Will, Mind, and Emotion), and lives in a Body.

> **Man is created with a higher matter than the earth; hence, man can easily dominate everything. Man is a Spirit, has a Soul (the seat of your Will, Mind, and Emotion), and lives in a Body.**

Your Spirit lives forever, beyond this world. Your soul is you; your will, your intellect is formed as you grow and explore this world. Your body is your physical presentation, the package that connects you to others through your senses. This body dies when you die. It belongs to this earth, it is earthly, and it fades away.

Your Spirit influences your soul, and your soul influences your body. These three parts of man can also decide independently, as seen by many that train their body beyond normal to do extreme exercises. There are a lot of mental training that can lead to an intensive supernatural world and experiences. The Spirit can also be so indulged that humanity becomes spiritually aligned, and such a person work many miraculous works.

The Spirit, the soul and the body can also work separately against their norm to become disharmonized. This disharmony is what brings about op-press, de-press and dis-ease.

The Spirit can be oppressed; this is the default state of all humanity. The soul: Mind, Brain, Emotion also can be de-pressed, leading to mental depression and all manner of mental ill conditions as seen today. The body also can be dis-eased, as seen with the flooding of all manner of sicknesses and diseases of humanity today.

MAN RELATES AT THE THREE LEVELS OF BEING.

Man is triune. Man is a Spirit, has a Soul (seat of Will, Mind and Emotion), and lives in a Body. Man relates at these three levels of being, Spiritually, at the Soul (Intellectually, Mentally, Wilfully, Emotionally), and Physically; Expressing the emotional inclinations through the sense of touch, sight, taste, feel and hear.

Natural man makes decisions at these various levels of being too. Understanding this triune nature of man is key to making significant decisions in life.

These different levels of being are why a Man can be very connected to some people based on business connectivity alone. The same man will have a prophet or spiritual guide to which he is highly loyal; while connecting to others for sexual satisfaction alone; and others based on commitment such as family ties or social responsibilities.

These connections simultaneously operate because man relates to these seemingly unrelated people through his triune being connectivity.

MAN DEVELOPS AT DIFFERENT LEVELS OF BEING.

Man develops at different levels of being. Man can independently train and establish themselves at the different levels of being, spiritually, mentally, emotionally and physically.

Spiritually, man is sold to the rule of darkness and at their mercy as a default. When a man is born again, he is translated into the kingdom of Christ. This deliverance is through the forgiveness of his sins by the Blood of Jesus Christ. Other than this, every other religious inclination simply modifies the man's soul and character, not the Spirit.

At the Soul level, man develops mentally and intellectually. Some informally through family and societal exposure, culture, and heritage. The man also develops formally through schooling, education, information technology, training, apprenticeship, mentoring, etc. There is also the exploitation of the Mind. Today, there are many mind training, deep and advanced training, a high realm of soul building; many are engaging this today to attract many things to themselves.

Physically, men can also control and train themselves in Eating, Exercising, Bodybuilding, Physical training, Skill-building, etc. Today, many stars are born purely from engaging in physical exercises of their body, entertaining and manifesting in many capacities that hitherto would not have been possible to ordinary people. Many have made a great fortune from such activities and abilities.

MAN OPERATES AT THESE VARIOUS LEVELS.

As with the development and relating, man also operates and makes ends meet and earn a living at these different levels of being,

Physically, this is the least level. At this level, people work based on their physical abilities, based on their strength and stamina. Working at this level, when such a one is not available, such as being on holiday, ill, indisposed for any reason, no work is done. This level consists mainly of the employee.

Mentally, many people fall into this category. Here, a form of training is required to be a skilled worker. Depending on the degree of skills and expertise acquired, the scale, status and remunerations varies.

Here you find the graduates, specialists, and qualified personnel; this set of people knows how to do things. With them, they are equally time-bound; when they are not around, their work stops! However, they are similarly mainly employees with higher pay depending on the skill or expertise they have.

Some men operate at the spiritual, or better still called intuitive and insightful level. This level is working based on a higher understanding of a purpose. These people ask and know the why of a thing. They understand the purpose of a business. They are mainly employers of labour. For them, work go on even when they are absent. They build systems, engage the experts, engage the physically capable people, and leverage other people's brains and time for profit. These are the CEOs, the Heads of Organizations, and the Owners of Businesses.

In choosing a life partner, man also tends to relate to these various levels of being. Many choose based on physical attractions only; some choose based on mental or intellectual connectivity, whereas there is also a realm of choosing based on your spiritual inclination.

Because many people are not conscious of their triune nature, they tend to base their life decisions on physical and mental judgement alone. However, the correct order of things is that you are a spirit being; you influence the soul, which controls the body. When these three are not in harmony, tension is created. A lot of stress and anxiety over the mind and the body could lead to depression, mental oppression, diseases and body malfunctioning. In the beginning, it was not so!

WHY THE BOUNDARIES IN CHOOSING LIFE PARTNERS IN THE KINGDOM OF CHRIST.

Although we are in this world, living, working and doing business with everyone around, however, we are not the same with the ungodly and unbelievers. What society accept as correct may not be the same as what the Bible says. **We are believers, and we choose to stand on the Word of God, on all issues, no matter what!**

Our body is the temple of the Most High, The day we receive Jesus Christ as our Lord and Saviour; His Spirit comes to reside in us, from that day forward, it is not about our views, it is now about the Word of God, allowing the Spirit of Christ in us operates through us. This way, our body becomes His temple; hence are to be referenced and treated accordingly. **We are not like everyone in the world; we are different. If anyone is in CHRIST, they are a new creature.**

'Therefore, if anyone is in Christ, he is a new creation; old things have passed away; behold, all things have become new.' (2 Corinthians 5:17 NKJV).

Let us see what our manual, the Bible says about the bodies of believers:

[15]*"know ye not that your bodies are the members of CHRIST? Shall I then take the members of CHRIST, and make them the members of an harlot? GOD forbid.* [16]*What? Know ye not that he which is joined to an harlot is one body? For two, saith he, shall be one flesh.* [17]*But he that is joined unto the Lord is one Spirit.* [18]*Flee fornication. Every sin that a man doeth is without the body; but he that committeth fornication sinneth against his own body.* [19]*What? Know ye not that your body is the temple of the Holy Ghost which is in you, which ye have of God, and ye are not your own?* [20]*For ye are bought with a price: therefore glorify God in your body, and in your Spirit, which are GOD's."* (1 Corinthians 6:15-20 KJV)

MAN AT SALVATION

Let us take a quick reminder of the Man (and woman) at Salvation. When a man is born again, his Spirit is re-united with his creator, not his soul or body. Your Spirit becomes united with the Spirit of God, the Spirit of Christ. Your soul was not born again; neither was your body born again. The transformation occurs only in your Spirit. Your mindset is still intact, your physique and looks untouched.

That is why many Christians still have capacities to continue in their evil deeds although their Spirit is born again. As highlighted above, the spirit rules, followed by the soul, and then the body. However, if the Spirit is not allowed to influence the Mind, a crisis can occur. The Bible called this being 'Carnal.' Carnality is being born again, yet allowing the unregenerated mind to dictate your actions; instead of the Holy Spirit. Such persons birth confusions in deeds and actions.

Ignoring this order does not change it; it is what is responsible for our outcome. Let us see some examples here; a professor in a life crisis, well-trained personnel yet highly diseased. A churchgoer yet oppressed with all manner of confusion and identity crisis. The list is on.

THE STATE OF YOUR SPIRIT.

The conforming of your soul, mind and intellect to your spirit and your body's submission to your inner being will determine your outcome in life. When a man gives his life to Our Lord, Jesus Christ,

> *The conforming of your soul, mind and intellect to your spirit and your body's submission to your inner being will determine your outcome in life.*

He, Jesus Christ, the life of God is introduced into his Spirit being; such a one becomes a new creature spiritually.

However, they need to spend time to learn more about this new life through the word of God and consciously submits his thoughts to obey the new nature in him: The Spirit of CHRIST. He is also to put his body under subjection, such as seen in constant fasting and disciplines. Engaging this will birth the true nature of CHRIST in him fully in the spirit, soul and body.

'Now may the God of peace Himself sanctify you completely; and may your whole spirit, soul, and body be preserved blameless at the coming of our Lord Jesus Christ.' (1 Thessalonians 5:23 NKJV)

I pray this prayer becomes our reality in the Name of YESHUA HAMASHIACH (JESUS CHRIST), Amen.

Even though our spirit becomes transformed as we receive CHRIST into our lives, we are expected to train and nurture our mind, soul, emotions, and body to align with our new nature in CHRIST.

The degree to which this is achieved will determine the extent of manifestations of the fullness of CHRIST we display here on earth.

'I beseech you therefore, brethren, by the mercies of God, that you present your bodies a living sacrifice, holy, acceptable to God, which is your reasonable service.

[2]And do not be conformed to this world, but be transformed by the renewing of your mind, that you may prove what is that good and acceptable and perfect will of God.' (Romans 12:1-2 NKJV)

THE BOUNDARIES IN CHOOSING LIFE PARTNERS.

We intentionally dealt extensively with the above to under-score the importance of man's true nature, especially in CHRIST. The most important part of your being when it comes to the boundaries in choosing marriage; is your Spirit.

This part of you is your authentic you. Your partner must share of same Spiritual source and connectivity.

Before considering other mental, intellectual, emotional, and physical compatibilities, the very first decision should be: 'Is their Spirit in unity with CHRIST? Because, eventually, the Spirit rules.

> *The most important part of your being when it comes to the boundaries in choosing marriage; is your Spirit. This part of you is your real you. Your partner must share of same Spiritual source and connectivity.*

A physically or mentally sound man or woman can be adversely influenced by his or her spiritual disposition anytime and any day.

When not surrendered to JESUS CHRIST as your Lord, you are under the rule of the forces of Darkness; Satan is in control, irrespective of the moral or mental soundness.

The devil has free access to their lives and can influence them negatively at any time. The enemy will surely take advantage of this opportunity to buffet the believers who marry unbelievers.

Who are you choosing as a life partner?

You can have friends at different levels. Your colleagues at work, your neighbours, your community or professional associations, even your family members. At various levels, such as physically. (Girls club, Men's club, teen's club), mentally (School mates, career, professional colleagues).

However, when it comes to Spirituality connectivity, these are beyond friends; they are family; hence you must pay close attention to those you bring close as your spiritual friends.

MARRIAGE IS A SPIRITUAL UNION. Where two becomes one. Spiritual connectivity is critical; hence, the scriptures warn us of choosing outside our spiritual boundary.

DO NOT BE UNEQUALLY YOKED WITH THE UNBELIEVERS.

Being 'Unequally Yoked' with an unbeliever allows the Spirit of God to unite with the force of darkness. This unequally yoked occurs when a Christ-filled Spirit (born again Christian) joins in marital intimacy with another that is not redeemed, whose spirit is still alienated from GOD and is therefore cursed and under the complete rule and control of the force of darkness.

This unequal yoked is the worst thing a man can do to himself. Irrespective of the mental or physical connectivity, you will be connected as spirit beings when you come together in a marital union. Therefore, when a spouse's spirit is not redeemed, it marries the opposing spirit, causing further confusion and chaos.

Let us see what the Bible says about this.

14Do not be unequally yoked together with unbelievers. <u>For what fellowship has righteousness with lawlessness? And what communion has light with darkness?" 15And what accord has CHRIST with Belial? Or what part has a believer with an unbeliever?" 16And what agreement has the temple of God with idols? For you are the temple of the living GOD.</u>

As God has said: "I will dwell in them and walk among them. I will be their GOD, and they shall be my people." 17Therefore "come out from among them and be separate, says the Lord. Do not touch what is unclean, and I will receive you." 18"I will be a father to you, and you shall be my sons and daughters, says the Lord Almighty." (2 Corinthians 6:14-18 NKJV)

Getting it right at this stage is very important. A man's outcome is his spiritual disposition. No matter how beautiful or handsome someone is, nor how educated, well mannered and tempered they present now, the spiritual disposition will take supremacy eventually, as to who rules over them!

When two persons with different spiritual dispositions come together, especially if one of them is redeemed in CHRIST JESUS, the enemy will capitalize on this gap to buffet the union now or in future, as the scriptures highlighted below:

[14]Do not be unequally yoked together with unbelievers. <u>For what fellowship has righteousness with lawlessness? And what communion has light with darkness?"</u> [15]<u>And what accord has CHRIST with Belial? Or what part has a believer with an unbeliever?"</u> [16]<u>And what agreement has the temple of God with idols? For you are the temple of the living GOD.</u>

As God has said: "I will dwell in them and walk among them. I will be their GOD, and they shall be my people." (2 Corinthians 6:14-16 NKJV)

> **A man's outcome is his spiritual disposition.**
>
> **No matter how beautiful or handsome someone is, nor how educated, well mannered and tempered they present now, their spiritual disposition will take supremacy eventually as to who rules over them.**

Getting it right at this point can never be overemphasized. This proper spiritual connectivity is because every other thing will be built upon this foundation.

The myth that 'He is a good and nice man, and he is already attending church with me,' or 'she likes me, and I will convert her' will not always work. No one can change another; if the unbeliever becomes converted, it is good, however, if they decide not to, no one can force them to, and the enemy can use this gap as a legal entrance into your family.

This proper connectivity is why GOD admonishes us to, at this choosing stage, to choose right, choosing within the boundary of Faith. Choosing only those who have given their lives to Jesus Christ, then you can be sure only CHRIST rules supremely over them.

That one chooses from the Church does not mean that there is no possibility of a marital crisis. Marital relationships are dynamic, and many factors are brought to the fore for a smooth ride. When two redeemed people come together, and they are willing to yield to the 3rd Person in Marriage, there will not be any problem, lack, ill background, incompatibility, or any crisis for that matter that will not be surmountable before them. For such a union between a Godly man, woman and GOD are not easily broken!

'And if one prevail against him, two shall withstand him; and a threefold cord is not quickly broken.' (Ecclesiastes 4: 12 KJV)

'And though one can overpower him who is alone, two can resist him. A cord of three strands is not quickly broken.' (Ecclesiastes 4: 12 AMP)

When the two persons in a marital relationship are redeemed and united with CHRIST, the 3rd Person in Marriage, The Spirit of God

Himself, will have free access to join the union, making it a formidable force against all forces of the enemy.

The price to choose right within the boundary of CHRIST will be one of the greatest gifts you ever give yourself in this world!

> *The price to choose right within the boundary of CHRIST will be one of the greatest gifts you ever give yourself in this world!*

Marriage is between a man, a woman and GOD. Hence being in the right standing with God will allow Him to function in your marriage. As we have emphasized in this book series, Marriage is not just between a man and a woman. Marriage is between a man, a woman, and GOD.

NOW THAT I HAVE CHOSEN WRONGLY.

As much as choosing right within the boundary of Faith in CHRIST is essential, many do not have this opportunity. Many already chose from outside the faith before receiving JESUS CHRIST as their Lord and Saviour.

Though churchgoers, tongue talkers and tithe payers, others chose from outside the Faith boundary due to lack of understanding of the spiritual implications or are simply overshadowed by the mental, moral and physical attributes of such partners, until when the realities of the spiritual disposition come taunting them. No matter why and how you find yourself in this state, now that you are in a marital relationship with a not redeemed partner, what is the way out of it?

Many relationships are purely contracted, based on mental and physical connectivities; many of them survive too; however, they risk being influenced by the forces of darkness any day and any time.

Things happen, such as ignorance of who we are in CHRIST; lack of adequate information on the consequences of wrong spiritual connectivity. Also, are pressure from peers, family and friends; the pressure of the world system for results and class; the direct or indirect influence of the force of darkness blindfolding people in oppression to choose wrongly…

Things do happen. Now that you know, Now that you find yourself here, what should you do? Is there a way out of these? Let us see some possible steps to take in handling the cause of this crisis in marriage.

- Repentance, confession and returning to GOD.

Such a person must make formal repentance and confession of this gravy sin, so the sin is no more speaking against them, no matter how long in such a marriage. For every unrepented, unconfessed, or covered sin will still be speaking against you, no matter how long ago you committed them!

'Though hand join in hand, the wicked shall not be unpunished: but the seed of the righteous shall be delivered.' (Proverbs 11:21 KJV)

'He who covers his sins will not prosper, But whoever confesses and forsakes them will have mercy.' (Proverbs 28:13 NKJV)

[18]"Come now, and let us reason together,' Says the Lord, 'Though your sins are like scarlet, They shall be as white as snow; Though they are red like crimson, They shall be as wool, [19]If you are willing and obedient, You shall eat the good of the land; [20]But if you refuse and rebel, You shall be devoured by the sword;' For the mouth of the Lord has spoken.' (Isaiah 1:18-19 NKJV)

- Acceptance and willingness to submit your will and marriage to GOD.

God gave man the honour of choosing and making decisions about their outcome in life. Many do not know this; hence, they are deceived into choosing against their will and desire. The Bible made this clear as follows:

[15]'See, I have set before you today life and good, death and evil,

[19]I call heaven and earth as witnesses today against you, that I have set before you life and death, blessing and cursing; therefore choose life, that both you and your descendants may live;' (Deuteronomy 30:15, 19 NKJV)

Man has a will to choose, the Spirit of God told me one day that:

'The abilities of Good is of God, the abilities of evil are of darkness; however, the Will to make a Choice is of Man, when a man makes a choice, the corresponding abilities back him. Now, man will be responsible for the choices he makes today and on the day of judgement. '

Pause, Ponder, and think about this!

Man has a will to choose. And what you do not choose is not permitted to happen to you. Many do not know when they choose an outcome; whenever you consent verbally or in thought to a thing's possibilities, you are already choosing such!

Hence, on this issue of managing the crisis of choosing wrongly, men have to consciously decide to submit to God's will and let GOD have the final say in their marriage.

As elaborated in this book, the 3rd Person in Marriage can work a customized miracle for any willing marriage actor. The question is, are you ready to allow GOD to step into your situation? His will may not be conventional.

God's decisions for you may not be similar to your neighbour's. However, His choice will always be in line with His Word and the revelation of Christ for your life.

Are you willing to accept and submit the will of God for your marriage? Think about this.

- A decision to do it right this time.

You will have to decide to do things right this time. In the earlier volume of this book series, The Preparations, we dealt extensively on the core characteristics of the first man and woman created, raising a Godly man and a Godly woman, and the three basic marriage laws: Love, Submission and Sexual Purity.

It is crucial to decide to do things right, not standing on your right or insisting your partner accept you for who you are. With the help of the 3rd Person in Marriage, you may have to make a conscious effort to work on your areas of weakness and do things right.

Engaging this self-help is a sure way of letting The 3rd Person in Marriage create a customised miracle and way out for your marriage. Please endeavour to check volume one of this book series and engage the exercises at the end of the book. Be sincere and diligent in these exercises, and *'if you are willing and obedient, you shall eat the good of the land.' (Isaiah 2:19 NKJV)*

- Aligning with GOD's will

You will have to decide to align with the will of God. This alignment is not just doing things because they are correct; beyond this, it is doing something because God says so. The Bible talks about the Good, acceptable and perfect will of God.

'And do not be conformed to this world, but be transformed by the

renewing of your mind, <u>that you may prove what is that good and acceptable and perfect will of God</u>.' (Romans 12:2 NKJV)

Beyond doing the right thing, the Spirit of God may give you more, a customized action to take that will cause the miracle of peace you so much desired in your marriage.

- Patiently follow as GOD turns things in your favour.

In your restoration and healing journey, patience is essential; many have had a shipwreck of their faith without this.

> **You will have to decide to align with the will of God. This alignment is not just doing things because they are correct; beyond this, it is doing something because God says so.**

[2]'My brethren, count it all joy when you fall into various trials, [3]knowing that the testing of your faith produces patience. [4]<u>But let patience have its perfect work, that you may be perfect and complete, lacking nothing</u>. [5]if any of you lack wisdom, let him ask of God, who gives to all liberally and without reproach, and it will be given to him.' (James 1:1-5 NKJV).

The journey requires patiently following as God turns things in your favour. He will, *'if you are willing and obedient, you shall eat the good of the land,'* says Isaiah 1:19.

The decision to heal and restore your home is not a popular virtue; the faster, deceptive, and easier route is to 'MOVE ON' and start a new relationship, assuming that the faults are always from the other partner. Acknowledging the 3rd Person in Marriage and recognizing His abilities to work a customized miracle for you should be your succour as you patiently follow as he turns things around in your favour.

- Obedience to the leading of GOD.

Choosing to be obedient to the leading of God even if your partner is not cooperating may be a call to take. Many contribute their part of the deal when there is a cooperation of others involved; this is the world's typical way.

In the kingdom of Christ, we are to be obedient to the leading of God, irrespective of the willingness and responsiveness of the other parties involved. Obedience to the leading of God is a personal decision to make, and it is very unconditional!

- There may be a demand for restitution.

In the journey of managing a crisis of wrong choices, there may be a demand for restitution; these may be some actions to re-address some of the issues. This step should be individual case-based and not just a general rule for all marital crises. If you align yourself properly with God and submit to His will, He will show you the steps you may need to take on the journey for a customized miracle for your marital destiny.

- There may be denials.

During this period, denial may come up; many may need to be alone, solo, and lonely while on this journey. There may be a denial of intimacy, pleasure, companionship and comfort.

Denials may not always be the case; however, some forms of denials may be required during this period. It is, therefore, essential to prepare and be willing to endure such denials for the season as you follow and see God, the 3rd Person in Marriage, turn things around in your favour.

- There may be long term waiting.

There may be a long waiting time; this as much as possible may not be encouraged or promoted; however, individual circumstances vary. If demand for long-term waiting is placed on you in the course of your journey of restoration of your marital Bliss, confirmations that God is in the journey will make the journey so smooth; you will not even feel the time of waiting.

The bottom line is your willingness to allow God, the 3rd Person in Marriage, to step in to create a customized miracle for you.

Will you engage in repentance, confession and returning to GOD? Will you accept and submit your will and marriage to GOD? Will you decide to do it right this time? Are you ready to align with GOD's will, patiently following as GOD turns things in your favour?

Will you choose Obedience to the leading of GOD, willing to accept the demand for restitution, denials, and long term waiting, if need be?

Humanly speaking, the easier route of moving on to a new relationship is always preferred.

If your weight and burden remain intact on the journey of faith, no soothing and rest from God, there is a problem with your approach. Walking in line with Christ will always lead to rest for your souls.

However, understanding that the attack against your marriage is beyond the two parties involved; understanding that the willingness to honour God's covenant in Marriage is weightier than the journey will encourage one to take on the journey of restoring your home.

For anyone choosing to honour God, peace and comfort of the Holy Ghost are assured, and it will be as though there was no burden at all. Our Lord Jesus Christ says:

28'Come to Me, all you who are labor and are heavy laden, and I will give you rest. 29Take My yoke upon you, and learn from Me, for I am gentle and lowly in heart. And you will find rest for your souls. 30For My yoke is easy and My burden is light.' (Matthew 11:28-30 NKJV).

Yes, it is some work; however, this work of faith will turn the other labour and burden into 'Rest in God.' Think about this!

If your weight and burden remain intact on the journey of faith, with no soothing and rest from God, there is a problem with your approach. Walking in line with Christ will always lead to rest for your souls.

Marriage is one of the main routes the enemy attacks people because attacks from a spouse affect humanity's core; spiritually, mentally, socially, emotionally and physically. When couples are submitted to CHRIST, marriage becomes easier to manage and blissful; any journey's crisis will be dealt with together in faith.

Physical attraction comes up and down; it is not consistent. Mental interests may change based on the season of the couples' lives; however, your spiritual connectivity will always be alive. since it is aligned to God, who is more significant than you and the world.

Some unbelievers may experience marital bliss based on their mental or physical connectivity for some time, until if and when the force of darkness is ready to strike them!

As Christians, breaking an edge at this junction unlocks the enemy's attacks, who takes advantage of the unequally-yoked to buffet them!

Your Notes . . .

Why does one need boundaries in choosing for marriage? What are these boundaries?

Now that one had chosen wrongly, what are some steps to birth a customized way out of the crisis?

The 3rd
Person in
Marriage

WHEN TO

CHOOSE FOR

MARRIAGE

5. WHEN TO CHOOSE FOR MARRIAGE···

WHEN TO CHOOSE. ARE YOU READY FOR MARRIAGE?

Why engaging the scriptures for issues on marriage and not just on common sense?

"Then his disciples asked him, saying, "What does this parable mean?" And He said, "To you it has been given to know the mysteries of the kingdom of God, but to the rest it is given in parables, that 'seeing they may not see, and hearing they may not understand.' (Luke 8:9-10 NKJV)

The uniqueness of the scriptures is a bonus to anyone who uses engages it for their life and destiny!

"All scripture is given by inspiration of God, and is profitable for doctrine, for reproof, for correction, for instruction in

righteousness, that the man of God may be complete, thoroughly equipped for every good work." (2 Timothy 3:16-17 NKJV)

All scriptures are by inspiration of the HolySpirit, and can only be accessed with the help of the HolySpirit.

"Therefore I also, after I heard of your faith in the Lord JESUS and your love for all the saints, do not cease to give thanks for you, making mention of you in my prayers: that the GOD of our Lord JESUS CHRIST, the father of glory, may give to you the Spirit of wisdom and revelation in the knowledge of him, the eyes of your understanding being enlightened; that you may know what is the hope of his calling, what are the riches of the glory of his inheritance in the saints, and what is the exceeding greatness of his power toward us who believe, according to the working of his mighty power" (Ephesians 1:15-19 NKJV)

When to choose for marriage? Are you ready? Beyond your readiness physically and mentally, it is imperative to discover yourself spiritually before deciding on marriage.

DISCOVER YOU.

Do you know who you are in CHRIST? Are you submissive to Christ in your spirit, soul, and body? This discovery can come at any adult age; some people develop faster than others and take on life responsibilities earlier. When to choose is not mainly based on specific adult age; it is about discovering yourself. What are the key things to discover before deciding on Marriage? Let us see these below.

DISCOVER YOUR KEY PURPOSES.
I. Discover your purpose in life:

In preparing for marriage, it is vital to discover your purpose in life, Identify your gifts, and Identify your potentials. These may not need to be in full bloom or fully manifested; however, you must have some clarity about your purpose in life.

This step is easy; if you engage God as an individual, God reveals purposes to men and women inclined towards Him. The Bible says of the Spirit of Truth, The Holy Ghost; He specialises in revealing things to come, so we are not in complete darkness as to our journey in life.

[12]'I still have many things to say to you, but you cannot bear them now. [13]However, when He, the Spirit of truth, has come, He will guide you into all truth; for He will not speak on His own authority, but whatever He hears He will speak; and He will tell you things to come.' (John 16:12-13 NKJV)

As you incline yourself to the Lord, as an adult, the Holy Ghost, your Helper, will begin to reveal to you many things that pertain to life and Godliness, including your glorious purpose in life.

Another essential thing to know before deciding on marriage is to discover your purpose in marriage. It is very apt to its success.

II. Discover your purpose in marriage.

Another essential thing to know before deciding on marriage is to discover your purpose in marriage.

Today, many assume that marriage aims to belong, show forth, boost, show how much one can express themselves; based on lessons from the schools, community, social media, and peer pressure.

> *When your purpose in Marriage is clear, you know what you are bringing to the table, it becomes easy to ride the boat called Marital Bliss.*

The World system defines marriage in many perverse ways; however, there is a clear-cut purpose for the man in marriage and the woman in marriage in the kingdom of Christ. We dealt extensively with this in volume one of this Book series. The 3rd Person in Marriage: The Preparations. Let us remind ourselves again.

The man's basic characteristics in marriage are Dominion and Authority, Vision and Direction, and Stability. Similarly, there are three basic characteristics of the woman in marriage: Smartness and Intuition; Influence, and Beauty.

Beyond these characteristics, there is the making of the Godly man and the Godly woman according to scriptures.   Marriage is not just between a man and a woman; Godly marriage is a union between a man, a woman and God, (the 3rd Person in Marriage).

When your purpose in Marriage is clear, you know what you are bringing to the table, it becomes easy to ride the boat called Marital Bliss. It is, therefore, vital to discover your purpose in marriage. Lack of understanding of this purpose has been the cause of many crises and pain in marriage and life.

III. Discover your purpose in a Godly relationship.

Finally, there are three cross-cutting laws of marriage: Love, Submission, and Sexual Purity. These can constitute the ideal purpose of marriage in the kingdom of Christ. These laws are not restricted to only the male or the female; they are cross-cutting, the man has his place in them, the woman has her place in them; adhering to these laws is key to Marital Bliss.

Now that we have addressed the need to discover you and your purpose in life, Christ, and marriage, let us now see how our guide, the first man, Adam, was made ready for marriage. They are all there, in those scriptures!

[7]Dr Myles Munroe had elaborated teachings on this area, using this same scriptural story of the first man and woman to discover when it is good to decide for marriage. Let us look into this.

---

[7] Dr Myles Munroe. www.munroeglobal.com

OPERATING IN YOUR GARDEN.

To be ready for marriage, there must be a provision path for the couple. Financial intelligence and fruitfulness are critical to managing a home. Do you have a job, a skill, or an ability currently fetching you income to sustain a family? Are you financially ready for marriage?

Our scriptural reference revealed that Adam was already working and operating in his garden before his marriage. This financial freedom is especially very important for the Man to be in marriage. The scriptures made it very clear that a man must fend for his household; **providing for the family is vital as an essential aspect of marriage readiness.**

[15]'*Then the Lord God took the man and put him in the garden of Eden to tend and keep it.* [16]*And the Lord God commanded the man, saying, "of every tree of the garden you may freely eat,* [17]*but of the tree of the knowledge of good and evil you shall not eat, for in the day that you eat of it you shall surely die."* [18]*And the Lord God said, "it is not good that man should be alone; I will make him a helper comparable to him."* [19]*Out of the ground the Lord God formed every beast of the field and every bird of the air and brought them to Adam to see what he would call them. And whatever Adam called each living creature, that was its name.* [20]*So Adam gave names to all cattle, to the birds of the air, and to every beast of the field. But for Adam there was not found a helper comparable to him.' (Genesis 2: 18-20 NKJV)*

The order of events is apparent from the above scripture: Adam got his job, *'Then the Lord God took the man and put him in the Garden of Eden to tend and keep it.'* Adam got a direction for life, a purpose for life, including what to do and not to do.

"of every tree of the garden you may freely eat, [17]but of the tree of the knowledge of good and evil you shall not eat, for in the day that you eat of it you shall surely die.".

Then, Adam resumed work at his job, he named all the creatures, took control, worked with God, for a divine purpose, *'So Adam gave names to all cattle, to the birds of the air, and to every beast of the filed'.* All of these before a need for a companion! *'But for Adam there was not found a helper comparable to him.'*

Worth noting also is that God identified the need for Adam's companionship long before him. After God had settled Adam in his job, purpose and vocation, God knew that Adam needed a companion; however, He pathed a course so that Adam could see this need himself.

When to choose in Marriage... **Through our Helper, the Holy Ghost, God Almighty knows when you are prepared and ready for marriage and will prompt you for this at the right time.** Today, many just decide on marriage simply because everybody is into it, the family and community, or peer pressures are demanding. However, if you submit yourself to God and are inclined with the

108

Holy Ghost, He will sort you out first, put you in your Garden, and grant you your vocation so that you will be well prepared to handle it when marriage comes along.

As much as timing is key for the man in marriage, God also prepares the woman for the right timing. We will get to this in the subsequent chapter.

The scripture makes it clear that man, as the head, must provide for his household. This responsibility does not preclude the woman's support; however, a man must be ready financially to sustain his head in the family. The family needs 'bread', hence 'bread' must be provided. When a man fails at this, the woman naturally steps in as the 'Breadwinner', which has led to several abuse cases in the family.

The scripture is very clear on this. Man must provide for his household. We pray that the Grace to break through financially to care for your household is granted unto you as a man in the Name of YESHUA HAMASHIACH (Jesus Christ), Amen.

"But if anyone does not provide for his own, and especially for those of his household, he has denied the faith and is worse than an unbeliever." (1 timothy 5:8 NKJV)

Women as the helpmeet are to learn to manage resources. Today, education and civilization open the door for women to be financially independent; it is essential to allow the man to provide for the household while the woman supports.

109

When things are done right, according to the original manual of the marriage institution, The Biblical counsel, then we get the desired marital bliss. However, doing things our way and expecting a blissful outcome is unrealistic and very difficult to attain. This is why we see many marriages starting well and from nowhere, heading for divorce.

The scripture describes a Godly woman concerning financial management as follows:

'Who can find a virtuous wife? For her worth is far above rubies.' *(Proverbs 31:10 NKJV)*

See the Amplified Bible rendition this: *'An excellent woman [one who is spiritual, capable, intelligent, and virtuous], who is he who can find her? Her value is more precious than jewels and her worth is far above rubies or pearls.' (Proverbs 31:10 AMP).*

When women support, it brings all of the woman's smartness to fore in the home's management, *'one who is spiritual, capable, intelligent, and virtuous.'* Think about this. Let us see more below as the scriptures encourage Godly women *'to be discreet, chaste, homemakers, good.'*

3'The older women likewise, that they be reverent in behavior, not slanderers, not given to much wine, teachers of good things—4that they admonish the young women to love their husbands, to love their children, 5to be discreet, chaste, homemakers, good, obedient to their own husbands, that the word of God may not be blasphemed." (Titus 2:3-5 NKJV)

All of these attributes are not absolute age determined. As marriage is not for babies or young boys and girls, maturity comes faster for some and slower for others. Thus, beyond the attainment of the bare adult age, maturity must be considered individually. Are you ready for a relationship?

The question is, are you ready for marriage? Do you know who you are, not who daddy and mummy say you are; Do you have an insight into your purpose in life? Are you fruitful in your work? Are you successfully taking up responsibilities in other areas of life? Do you have a purpose that requires a helpmeet? Are you ready to love as GOD prescribed? Are you prepared to submit as unto the Lord? Or are you just driven by your emotional, sexual arousal and stirring?

Think and ponder on these things, for the place of preparations can never be over-emphasized; if you prepare well for your marriage, you are propping yourself for a better outcome.

I have no right; I obtain GOD's mercies through our Lord, JESUS CHRIST. My dear friend, what will you instead do with this information? Are you ready for marriage?

Your Notes . . .

When is the right time to choose for marriage?

Your Notes.

What are the key purposes of life you should discover before choosing for marriage?

The 3rd Person in

ENGAGING

THE DIVINE

HELPERS

6. ENGAGING THE DIVINE HELPERS···

ENGAGING THE DIVINE HELPER.

*A*braham, the patriarch of faith, living in the promised land, Canaan, having worked with GOD and saw the differences between living under the covenant of GOD's Blessing and labour, toil and curse, as seen in the lives of the rest of the people around him. He made his servant swear that he would not marry a wife for his covenanted son, the heir of the promise: Isaac, from the heathen that lived around him in Canaan land.

'Now Abraham was old, well advanced in age; and the Lord had blessed Abraham in all things. ²So Abraham said to the oldest servant in his house, who ruled over all that he had, "Please put your hand under my thigh, and I will make you swear by the Lord, the God of heaven and the God of the earth, that you will not take

a wife for my son from the daughters of the Canaanites, among whom I dwell; 3but you shall go to my country and to my family, and take a wife for my son Isaac.'' (Genesis 24:2-3 NKJV)

Esau, the first son of Isaac, took two wives of the heathen. They became a burden to his parents, so much that when Esau saw that Jacob, his brother was to go to a faraway country, among their parents' former nation, to marry a wife, Esau decided to pick the third wife from the Ishmaelite. He sought a nearer relative to partake of a touch of God's Blessing in the new wife. (Genesis 28:6-9)

Why engage the divine helper? Why do we not choose purely based on our feelings, mental connectivity and social connectivity? This pattern is what the world system and 'society correctness' had accepted as standard; however, in the Kingdom of Christ, it is different; we are not of this world, though living in the world, our ways of life and values are different. We are quickened-spirit beings with the capacity of Christ on this earth.

Our Lord Jesus Christ, preparing to depart this world, prayed for His disciples and all who will become believers after them; you and I, praying that God should keep us from the evil one of the world.

15'I do not pray that You should take them out of the world, but that You should keep them from the evil one. 16They are not of the world, just as I am not of the world. 17Sanctify them by Your truth, Your word is truth.' (John 17: 15-17 NKJV)

Understanding these different kingdoms is key to a victorious Christian life. We, as individuals, relate, love and care for many; our family members, neighbours, colleagues, business partners, schoolmates, and all. However, it is very important to know that all these acquaintances are not our 'spiritual family' as long as they are not believers; and had not made our Lord Jesus Christ their Lord and Saviour.

Therefore, they must not be kept at a too close reach in all situations, of course, until they become believers and understands prioritizing the Lordship of Christ in their lives.

> **Sentiment aside, soundness of mind aside, as long as they are not 'born again', Satan is the lord of their lives and can easily stand on their gates of influence over your life to buffet you.**

Sentiment aside, soundness of mind aside, as long as they are not 'born again', Satan is the lord of their lives and can easily stand on their gates of influence over your life to buffet you.

In choosing for marriage, this difference of kingdoms become significant. However, once you are in the habit of not making very close acquaintances with unbelievers, no matter who they are, either as family members, friends, colleagues, etc. It becomes easy not to seek a marital partner from them.

In the previous chapter, we dealt extensively with the boundary of choosing, highlighting its importance and encouraging not to be unequally yoked with unbelievers.

Schools, Market place, office places, and neighbourhoods may bring many sweet and great memories; however, care must always be taken to remember that we are not of this world, hence need to keep ourselves with the help of God, so the evil one does not get at us. This point is vital. No matter how great that family member, neighbour, schoolmate, colleague, or business partner looks or sounds if they are not born again, they are not members of your new family, Christ kingdom!

> *'He who walks with wise men will be wise, But the companion of fools will be destroyed.'*
>
> *(Proverbs 13:20 NKJV)*

When we trust God in faith to keep us from the evil one, He will guide us and lead us to great friends and families inside the Kingdom of Christ. However, when we become indifferent about the different kingdoms in this world, that also is a choice; we become unequally yoked with unbelievers at many levels.

This choice is yours to take. For every pleasure, vocation, business and area of experts have representatives of the sons of God. Believe for this, and your very friends and close acquaintants will only be among the believers!

119

'He who walks with wise men will be wise, <u>But the companion of fools will be destroyed</u>.' (Proverbs 13:20 NKJV)

'Be not deceived: <u>evil communications corrupt good manners</u>.' (1 Corinthians 15:33 KJV)

'Do not be deceived: <u>Evil company corrupts good habits</u>.' (1 Corinthians 15:33 NKJV)

Think about this. Believe for friends among believers, ask God for this, and it will be your reality in life.

Beyond making friends and acquaintances among believers, choosing for marriage is even more profound. Even among the seemingly great believers around you, choosing for marriage requires much more than acquaintances because compatibilities are very important. In this world full of deceptions, especially in the church, we need divine help choosing marriage.

Because that man or woman is a Christian, goes to church, is active in church, in leadership in the church, looks and acts decent, and is good-tempered, it will not be enough for choosing such a one for marriage. They may be masking pieces of stuff that can be harmful to living together in future or may simply not be compatible with your personality in total.

These uncertainties are why we will be looking into the importance of engaging Divine Helpers in choosing for marriage.

WHY INVOLVE THE DIVINE HELPERS?

Earlier, we discussed the man's different makeup, as a spirit being, with a soul; the seat of will, mind and emotion, and lives in a body, the physical presentation. We also now know that man relates at these different levels. Moreover, the background and upbringing have a lot to do with perceptions and values formation. Therefore, it is impossible to know someone's totality just because you see them at a session of their life.

Man can mask weaknesses and ill manners for a season; therefore, engaging Divine Helpers can never be over-emphasized in deciding for marriage. Many that trivialize this opportunity do so to their peril. A simple check from your Divine Helper can make a world of difference in marriage outcome!

> *Man can mask weaknesses and ill manners for a season; therefore, engaging Divine Helpers can never be over-emphasized in deciding for marriage.*

While taking on this series, two essential Divine Helpers came out clearly: The Holy Ghost Himself and the organized marriage counselling teams in local churches. Let us quickly look at these Divine Helpers.

THE DIVINE HELPER -THE HOLY SPIRIT.

The Holy Ghost is the individually based Divine Helper. As a believer, you are to be led by the Spirit continually and in everything. Your helper, the HolySpirit, is given you to profit withal. Not engaging the HolySpirit in all of your life affairs will short-change you because not everything is spelt out in the scriptures.

However, with the Holy Spirit's help, you will see the details of all you need about life and Godliness from the scriptures through the inspiration of the Holy Spirit. The Holy Spirit knows you much more than you know yourself and loves you sincerely; hence He knows the best partner anyone can have in life journey.

Our Lord JESUS CHRIST, while rounding up His ministry here on earth, said in John chapters 14, 15 and 16 that *'It is important that I go away, For if I do not go, Neither will the helper comes to you. However when I go, My father will send the Helper, Who will show you things to come, Who will reveal My will to you.'*

The Holy Ghost is here on earth for a purpose; to be our helper here on earth. The Holy Ghost, called in Greek as The Paraclete, translated as Comforter, Teacher/Counsellor, Advocate, Intercessor, Strengthener, and Standby.

These attributes manifest when needs arise. Comforting, teaching and guiding into all truth, advocating for us in the face of battle, praying for and with us when we are weak or unsure what to pray about, strengthening us in our weakness and

standby when we cannot match up! Pause, Ponder and Think about this!

The scripture is very clear on issues such as 'You shall love God with all your heart.' 'Love your neighbour as yourself.' 'Do not commit adultery.' etc. However, there is nowhere you will find plainly 'Tomowo, you are to marry Bunmi.' Tomowo, I want you to work at the World Bank this year.' 'I want you to wear this suit to work today,' and so on.

This nitty-gritty of everyday life affairs is where the Holy Ghost steps in to guide us aright! As you follow and obey the scriptures in many things, He will also guide and direct you in areas and issues that may seem not precise or well spelt out in the scriptures. However, you have to start with the scriptures; you will understand God more, leading you in other things will become easy.

An example is when a believer is faced with two or more suitors of note, all well behaved and Christians; who will you choose? Holy Ghost, your Divine Helper, can step in and show you more profound things and why you should choose one instead of the others. Do you understand?

When you engage the Holy Ghost in your day-to-day life choices, especially in your marriage choice, He becomes your Guide and a Divine Helper indeed!

HOW DO WE ENGAGE THE HELP OF THE HOLY GHOST IN CHOOSING FOR MARRIAGE.

[8]Brother Kenneth E. Hagin has elaborated teachings on 'How to be led by the Spirit of God.' His teachings are available in the public domain, on social media, and in Books; please endeavour to lay your hands on these resources; they will indeed Bless you.

He said that *'the inner witness we experience, when the Holy Ghost gives us the go-ahead in life issues, is much more trustworthy, and reliable than numerous dreams, visions, revelations and prophecies.'* As believers, our spirits are united with Christ, alive, not corrupted, and will always agree with God's will. Our mind and body, however, need the training to conform to the will of God. Moreover, these other supernatural experiences, such as dreams, visions, revelations, or prophecies, are not exclusive to the spirit realm's light zone.

> *'Many miss the Divine visitation because of the supernaturals!'*
>
> *-Brother Kenneth E. Hagin*

The forces of darkness are also spiritual and have the capacities for dreams, visions, revelations, prophecies, signs and miracles.

---

[8] Kenneth E. Hagin. www.rhema.org

Therefore, relying solely on these supernatural occurrences can and are misleading in many ways. Brother Hagin says. *'Many miss the Divine visitation because of the supernaturals!'*

THE INNER WITNESS.

The inner witness is that simple 'green light', a 'go-ahead', conviction, and assurance we experience in our heart, not on our head region, somewhere around our belly area. An unexplainable peace always accompanies it. It is the most reliable way the Spirit of God leads the believers.

Some people describe this as *'something was telling me to do this or not to'*. Some expressed it as *'I just have that peace that this is what to do'*. Others describe the inner witness as *'I was simply excited about this as 'this is it'*.

As long as you are a believer., actively engaging the presence of God daily, and regarding the Word of God as your final authority in your life, then that simple, not-too-pushy, peaceful, inner witness, or inner knowing, can and should be trusted, always!

'The Spirit Himself bears witness with our spirit that we are children of God,' (Romans 8:16 NKJV)

The Holy Spirit, Your Divine Helper, always bears witness with your spirit on issues of life. Let us see how the Amplified Bible put this same scripture:

'The Spirit Himself testifies and confirms together with our spirit [assuring us] that we [believers] are children of God.' (Romans 8:14 AMP)

The Holy Spirit, your Divine Helper, always testifies, confirms together with your spirit, assures you on life issues, including choosing for marriage! Pause, Ponder and think about this!

[6]'This is He who came by water and blood —Jesus Christ; not only by water, but by water and blood. <u>And it is the Spirit who bears witness, because the Spirit is truth.</u> [7]For there are three that bear witness in heaven: the Father, the Word, and the Holy Spirit; and these three are one. [8]And there are three that bear witness on earth: the Spirit, the water, and the blood; and these three agree as one.' (1 John 5:6-8 NKJV)

The Holy Spirit do bear witness, testifying, confirming together with your spirit, assuring you on the issues of life!

For unbelievers or those not as committed to their walk with God may have a non-submissive mind, and the enemy can deceive them with floods of thoughts mimicking the right thing to do and become doom afterwards.

Many also put on a fleece, 'God, if it is your will that I marry Mr A or Ms B, let him wear a red shirt to church tonight, let her bring me a flask of food today.' Just like the other supernatural manifestations, fleece is not exclusive of the kingdom of Christ;

hence can be influenced by the forces of darkness. Many set up fleece and stepped out of the will of God for their lives!

The Divine Helper wants to help you indeed. 'God is not an author of confusion but of Peace'. However, it is essential to learn and practice being led by God's Spirit regularly and every day. When it is time to make significant and vital life decisions, such as who to be a marriage partner, it will not be challenging to recognize the leading of God.

'For as many as are led by the Spirit of God, these are the sons of God.' (Romans 8:14 NKJV)

We can never make it right without our Divine Helper in this life. He sees more, knows more, yet loves us, and has our utmost interest at heart; He also knows our weaknesses and who can tolerate them. He wants to lead us aright in all things, bearing witness with our spirit in the simplest way we can relate.

Because of the Holy Spirit's simplicity in leading and guiding through the inner witness, many Christians followed His leading and experienced great success in many things. However, because they did not know or understand that He was the one at work, they could not replicate this help in all circumstances, especially when they price the situation very serious and crucial. Many expect supernatural experiences from the Holy Spirit to know God's will for issues of high value to them. No, He will still lead us in His usual simple, inner witness approach!

After they fail, many often say. 'And something was telling me not to do this, not to take that, not to go there, not to. Not to.' Such persons were waiting for the supernaturals and missed the Divine Help!

'Jesus answered and said to them, 'You are mistaken, not understanding the scriptures nor the power of God.' (Matthew 22:29 NKJV)

> ***Many expect supernatural experiences from the Holy Spirit to know God's will for issues of high value to them.***
>
> ***No, He will still lead us in His usual simple, inner witness approach!***

Now you know, 'happy art thou' for engaging Him in all situations of life. The INNER WITNESS. Your sure guide in Life!

As Holy Ghost leads you in your simple day to day choices; He will guide you in seemingly 'very important,' 'urgent', or 'crucial' issues of life, in the same way, using the simple, not pushy, soft, inner witness, always accompanied with PEACE! Pay close attention and choose to follow this authentic and highly reliable way of knowing the will of God in all areas of life. The Holy Spirit will always align with the Word of God and will not contradict the Word. Hence, acquainting yourself with the Word of God more will endear you

128

to the Holy Spirit, who is the Spirit of Truth, the Divine Helper, bearing witness with our spirits.

THE DIVINE HELPER -THE CHURCH COMMITTEE ON MARRIAGE/ PRE MARITAL

There are great marital preparatory classes in most congregations. This program is where basic requirements and marriage standards are promoted among the flocks. Complexities and dynamics of local cultural influences are addressed while balancing the Word of God on marital issues.

Most local churches have this setup. There are also some seasoned marital counsellors and ministers that focus mainly on marriage and issues surrounding marriage. These services, either local-church-based or independently and interdenominational based marriage ministries, are Divine helpers concerning choosing in Marriage. The Bible encourages older women to teach the younger ones how to deal with marriage and life. So much knowledge can be transferred from the experienced ones to the younger couples.

[3]'The older women likewise, that they be reverent in behaviour, not slanderers, not given to much wine, teachers of good things- [4]that they admonish the younger women to love their husbands, to love their children, [5]to be discreet, chaste, homemakers, good, obedient to their own husbands, that the word of God may not be blasphemed.' (Titus 2:3-5 NKJV)

These committees create opportunities for the church to know the couples, creating a common platform for engaged couples to relate and form cordial attachments. They also help as checkmates for the couples.

Experienced and seasoned counsellors are assigned to the couples to dig into more aspects of the couple's lives to foster preparedness for marriage. This standard varies from church to church.

The marriage committees can also enforce standards such as checking for pre-marital sexual purity and health-related compatibilities like genotype. The committee can also venture in on the differences in culture. They can spot danger signs such as potential abusive relationships, deceptions, and insincerity from the engaged couples. They form a solid support for the betrothed in the face of resistance or crisis from one or both families.

Some of the marriage committees also cater for young couples, helping to address the immediate adjustments to married life such as sexual adjustment, welcoming of babies, financial adjustments and other incompatibilities.

Many people shy away from this opportunity and miss such support for their marriage as great as these divine helpers are! The enemy deceives many with the fact that the couples are not living in the same locations, hence cannot afford the meetings. Many hide under urgency that they need to get married quick, thus insisting on short marriage counselling sessions, preventing the counsellors' opportunity to help sort out some areas that could have been spotted and managed before entering into marriage.

The marriage counselling committee can take the form of organized coaching sessions, group classes with other intending couples, Live Questions and Answers sessions, outdoor activities and praying sessions. Such outreaches help build confidence among the engaged couples and create solid support for them, which they can lash upon in the future.

Even if your local church does not have such a robust marriage counselling committee, you are highly encouraged to seek such a service. Many independent, interdenominational ministries run such services in the church today. In case you are interested in this, we can help recommend such to you in your location. You could send us an email for details on this: info@air.church

Engaging these Divine Helpers help in many ways, and the benefits cannot be over-emphasized. As much as employing this support may not necessarily guarantee success in marriage, it can form a base of support for unions.

It is also encouraged that you do not skip classes or insist on short and quick sessions; as much as possible to you, engage these Divine helpers, as their dividends are great. Many questions, concerns and grey areas are addressed in these meetings, leading to a soft landing for new couples. Many examples of how other couples handle cases and issues are discussed.

Remember that Marriage is actively run here on earth; hence, the physical connectivity, cultural influences, and social norms are respected, even in the Church as believers. Engaging these specialized Divine Helpers, the Marriage counselling committee will go a long way in supporting marriages today.

Your Notes.

The Divine Helper -The HolySpirit: How can one engage Him in choosing for Marriage?

The Divine Helper -Engaging the marriage counselling committees: What are their benefits in choosing for marriage?

The 3rd Person in Marriage

3

...AND SHE SAID YES!

SAID YES!

7. ···AND SHE SAID, YES!

. . . AND SHE SAID, YES!

*M*an in his location. The woman positioned, and she said yes! Adam was in his position, Eve was positioned, and she said yes!

MAN IN HIS LOCATION.

Man is to be in his God's given location. (the centre of God's will) to find his suitable Mrs Helper! This location is not necessarily geographical; it is being at the centre of God's will for his life. And while at this location, God will position a woman to him that will suit this location. Let us take a closer look at how this was expressed in the marriage manual, the Bible. We addressed this in an earlier chapter; let us take a second look at it below:

Our scriptural reference in Genesis revealed that Adam was already working and operating in his garden before deciding on marriage.

[9]Dr Myles Munroe elaborated on this aspect extensively in some of his teachings. (These are available in the public domain).

Being at the centre of God's will is very important for the man aspiring to be in marriage. Let us see how God positioned Eve to Adam at his location:

Man is to be in his God's given location, to find his suitable Mrs Helper!

This location is not necessarily geographical; it is being at the centre of God's will for his life.

[15]*'Then the Lord God took the man and put him in the Garden of Eden to tend and keep it.* [16]*And the Lord God commanded the man, saying, "of every tree of the Garden you may freely eat,* [17]*but of the tree of the knowledge of good and evil you shall not eat, for in the day that you eat of it you shall surely die."* [18]*And the Lord God said, "it is not good that man should be alone; I will make him a helper comparable to him."* [19]*Out of the ground the Lord God formed every beast of the field and every bird of the air and brought them to Adam to see what he would call them. And whatever Adam called each living creature, that was its name.* [20]*So Adam gave names to all cattle, to the birds of the air, and to every beast of the field.*

But for Adam there was not found a helper comparable to him. *[21]And the Lord God caused a deep sleep to fall on Adam, and he slept; and He took one of his ribs, and closed up the flesh in its place.*

[22]Then the rib which the Lord God had taken from man He made into a woman, <u>and He brought her to the man</u>. [23]And Adam said: <u>'This is now bone of my bones And flesh of my flesh; She shall be called Woman, Because she was taken out of Man</u>.'' (Genesis 2: 18-23 NKJV)

The order of events is apparent from the above scriptures: Adam got his job, *'Then the Lord God took the man and put him in the Garden of Eden to tend and keep it.'* Adam got a direction for life, a purpose for life. including what to do and not to do. *''of every tree of the garden you may freely eat, [17]but of the tree of the knowledge of good and evil you shall not eat, for in the day that you eat of it you shall surely die.''*

Then, Adam resumed work at his job; he named all the creatures, took control, worked with God for a divine purpose. *'So Adam gave names to all cattle, to the birds of the air, and to every beast of the field'.* All of these before a need for a companion! *'But for Adam there was not found a helper comparable to him.'*

As usual, Adam was busy at his duty post, naming all the creatures God brought his way. One day, he was simply and casually at work when he saw the next creature to be named; however, beholding it (her), he knew intuitively that this one was different from all the other creatures he had been naming and dealing with, in the garden!

Immediately Adam proclaimed, *'This is now bone of my bones And flesh of my flesh; She shall be called Woman, Because she was taken out of Man.'*

Worth noting is that Adam was in his location when God positioned Eve to him. Not in a big parade, just in his usual regular day-to-day activities, and behold, the helpmeet was there!

> *The beauty of this is that she will be a helpmeet for your location when you find a woman at your location.*

The beauty of this is that she will be a helpmeet for your location when you find a woman at your location. Man's location is the centre of God's will for his life; every other passion or vocations are a mere season of his life. The actual location is the core of a man's personality. Meeting a woman at this location will fit the core; hence a suitable helpmeet for the man. Let us see some practical examples below:

An artist, having discovered his location and busy in his art, is ready for his helpmeet. While considering marriage, he took a vacation to explore his other passions like singing and joined a singing holiday cruise. At that camp, he found a lady dancer and decided to marry her. As good as this woman may seem, she is not a fit for his actual location; as she was not positioned at his core vision, she may not bring suitable help for his life.

A minister of the Gospel, called to sing, accepted his chosen path and already done some albums, is ready for choosing for marriage. However, he also has a side passion for mountain climbing and rural exploitation. One day, he took a two-week vacation with some friends to a faraway country to explore some mountains and wildlife. He met a sweet rural woman and decided to propose to her. Being not at his core location, this lovely woman positioned to him may not be a suitable meet for him.

A travelling missionary doctor that loves giving medical help to the less privileged, already on this path, is ready for marriage. One day, he heard of outreach for mission work; while on that outreach, he met this beautiful missionary woman visiting the camp from another mission work; he fell for her and proposed to her. Though they were both not in their physical locations, the man was a missionary doctor in his core location (missions). A woman positioned to him at that 'location' is a sure suitable helpmeet for him.

Can you spot the difference? Let us take one more case study:

An aspiring lecturer, loving to impact, had three masters, working in a bank, was busy with life, and was ready for marriage. One day, he went to get medications for a friend in a pharmacy store in his town; he fell in love with this beautiful God-fearing lady, an intelligent pharmacist and sound in education; he went all the way for her, and she said yes! This man, meeting an educated minded woman, is a rightly positioned and suitable helpmeet for him.

When men make decisions for marriage while exploring their 'side passions', they will always be attracted to women that may be suitable for that passion, however not ideal for the core of their purpose in life.

> *Women are solution carriers. As you identify your place in God, always remember that you are a solution hub, and your totality is to proffer solutions*

In choosing for marriage, the man is encouraged to be in his location, and the woman positioned, and she says yes! This order is key to finding a suitable helpmeet. Man in his location, woman to be positioned, and she said yes!

WOMAN TO BE POSITIONED.

Let us quickly focus on the woman. Yes, the woman is to be positioned. Does that mean women are not meant to have visions and purposes in life? Of course, they are. However, remembering the woman's essential characteristics, Smartness/Instinct,

Influence and Beauty, these traits are created to help. Women are solution hubs. Women are solution carriers. As you identify your place in God, remember that you are a solution hub, and your totality is to proffer solutions.

The question worth asking will now be where I am to offer my solutions. Who am I to help today, who am I to help for a lifetime, who qualifies for my solutions, who is worth my depth of solution hub? Understanding this will help to get the right partner.

Once the woman's identity is clear as a solution Hub, it is imperative to rely carefully and skilfully on God to link her or position her to the right man who needs her solutions. When a woman aligns herself to God fully, her multi-dimensional nature becomes the tool the Holy Spirit uses to influence her into being rightfully positioned.

A female doctor with inherent solutions for mission works, prompted by the Holy Ghost to accept an invitation for two weeks of mission outreach, and there, a missionary man spotted her!

A dancer with inherent skills in managing people and home keeper, prompted by the Spirit of God one day to pick up a job in a new hotel or club, and there the new hotel manager spotted her, and she became a solution hub for him!

A female veterinary doctor with a hectic schedule and an inherent love for animals may just be busy attending to a dog owner who happened to own an animal farm. She becomes the solution hub for him!

The Holy Spirit may lead a pretty lady to do a short image building for a firm. With her extensive social media presence, studded with sound communication skills, she attracted the firm's owner. In dare need of image building, the gentleman owning the firm loved her, and she became his solution hub!

> *When a woman aligns herself to God fully, her multi-dimensional nature becomes the tool the Holy Spirit uses to influence her into being rightfully positioned.*

The list is long. **As the woman aligns herself with God, she builds her capacity as an excellent solution hub and becomes submissive to God. The Holy Ghost can tweak some cords to position her to the man who will need her solution hub.**

Women are solution hubs built and ready to proffer solutions. As they align with God, they are positioned at suitable locations owned by men needing their peculiar solutions.

. . . AND SHE SAID YES!

Once a man is at his location and finds a woman positioned at that location, it is an excellent time to reach out to her. Any woman that likes you at your location is a suitable helpmeet for you. Any woman that sees you in your work dress, and loves you all the same, is likely to be a suitable helpmeet for you. To be sure, invite her to your location, not necessarily geographical, engage her in your vocations, and observe if this is home with her. Does she proffer solutions immediately as she steps into your domain; most likely, such a one is your suitable helpmeet.

Cautions: The solution hubs may come in the form of criticism, identifying weakness and lacuna in your core vocations, bear in mind, your solution hub may be in her raw state, hence just browsing all the areas that need your attention. She may be saying them out as insults, attacks or some uncultured way… Nevertheless, think about that!

> *Once a man is at his location and finds a woman positioned at that location, it is an excellent time to reach out to her.*
>
> *Any woman that likes you at your location is a suitable helpmeet for you.*

A man came to me some time ago, complaining that his wife was not good for him. He stormed: 'She opposed my vision, saying all manner of bad things about my capacity to run the vision I shared with her; she is not a good woman'. I calmed him down and shed some light on this.

'Your woman is your solution hub, though not skilled. When you shared your vision with her, she went to work, browsed your abilities, and remembered your strengths and weaknesses. She observed the available resources and the magnitude of your vision and downloaded all the areas that need attention. Unfortunately, these came off as insults and castigating your vision!

The man said: "hmmm... I did not think of it that way."

I further explained that if his wife were well trained, she would encourage you first and take those highlighted things to heart and pray about them. And with God, all of them would become your strengths! For her discoveries are correct, as bitter as they may sound!

Let us see another case; a man, who had been trying his luck for a bit, met this beautiful lady; challenging to get, eventually, one day, she accepted his invitation to his place. On getting there, she started instinctively arranging things and fixing things up; the dude said: 'This is my wife!'

Eve was positioned at Adam's location. Unfortunately, Adam decided to take a break from his core location; dressing the garden, he went to stand before the forbidden tree. This action was a wrong step. With his 'solution hub' beside him, she sure brought her solutions to the wrong place! Think about this. (Genesis 3:1-6)

The woman is to yield to the Spirit of God to be correctly positioned for her Mr Right! When the above conditions are altered: when a man searches for women, especially outside of his duty post (God's calling), he may attract a beauty; however, this may not be a suitable all seasons helpmeet for him.

In the same vein, when a woman stays rigid and unyielding to God's leading, she misses or delays the correct positioning to meet her Mr Right!

Flexibility is critical for the proper positioning of women. When a woman is flexible in submission to the Spirit of God, she may be led to do something unusual, go for dinner at that restaurant tonight, take that trip this month, go for that vacation this summer. Accept those invitations; engage this single club this season. Flexibility is

> *Man in his location, woman being positioned,*
>
> *. . . and she said yes!*

vital, as the Holy Spirit can have a free hand to position the woman with a man who needs her solution hub!

Man's location (centre of GOD's will) is critical in making the right choice in marriage.

Because God is the custodian of vision and direction, dominion and authority and stability, God empowered man to locate them!

146

A woman's yielding (For proper positioning) is key in meeting the right choice in marriage as the Spirit of God works through her instinct and smartness, influence and beauty!

A man taking a break from his duty post or not yet discovering his duty post will not meet his suitable help! A woman saying yes to a man, not in his location, is saying yes to the wrong man! Man in his location, woman being positioned, and she said yes!

We pray for grace for men to discover and stay busy at their GOD's given location in YESHUA HAMASHIACH's (Jesus Christ) Name, Amen. We pray for grace for women to be submissive to the Holy Spirit to be correctly positioned to meet their Mr Right in his duty post in YESHUA HAMASHIACH's (Jesus Christ) Name, Amen.

"He who finds a wife finds a good thing, and obtains favor from the Lord." (Proverbs 18:22 NKJV)

"Do we have no right to take along a believing wife, as do also the other apostles, the brothers of the Lord, and Cephas?" (1 Corinthians 9:5 NKJV)

"Search from the book of the Lord, and read: not one of these shall fail; not one shall lack her mate. For my mouth has commanded it, and his Spirit has gathered them." (Isaiah 34:16 NKJV)

You will not lack your mate in the Name of YESHUA HAMASHIACH (Jesus Christ), Amen.

Your Notes . . .

Man in his location, woman being positioned, and she said yes!
What are your thoughts about this?

Your Notes . . .

Man in his location, woman being positioned, and she said yes! Why are the proper location and rightful positioning important in choosing for marriage?

The 3rd Person in

3

INTRODUCING

THE MARITAL

MONSTER...

8. INTRODUCING THE MARITAL MONSTER···

INTRODUCING THE MARITAL MONSTER.

*I*n my course of taking on this series, in my journey in life as an individual, in my work in ministry, and as a LIFE Coach, I have seen a pattern of an attack, very peculiar oppression common in marriages, targeting mainly the simple, Godly, and the willing partners.

This oppression was eventually revealed to me as a demon, not just a low-level ranked demon; this is a principality, operating at the gate of influence against another. This evil spirit has some precise cut characteristics, is very peculiar and can oppress anyone, male, female, young, old, white, black, educated, uneducated, wealthy, poor, ministers, or church members. This demon can influence and oppress anyone!

152

The Bible talked about the gifts of the Spirit in Romans and First Corinthians; one of such gifts is Discerning of the Spirit.

4'There are diversities of gifts, but the same Spirit. 5There are differences of ministries, but the same Lord. 6And there are diversities of activities, but it is the same God who works all in all. <u>7But the manifestation of the Spirit is given to each one for the profit of all.</u> 8For to one is given the word of wisdom through the Spirit, to another the word of knowledge through the same Spirit, 9to another faith by the same Spirit, to another gifts of healings by the same Spirit, 10to another the working of miracles, to another prophecy, <u>to another discerning of spirits</u>, to another different kinds of tongues, to another the interpretation of tongues. 11<u>But one and the same Spirit works all these things, distributing to each one individually as He wills</u>.' (1 Corinthians 12:4-11 NKJV)

The Gift of the Discerning of spirits is a revelational gift that grants access into the details of the spirit behind a situation, such as seen when our Lord Jesus Christ addressed Satan through Peter when he invaded the body of Peter to distract Christ from His calling.

21'From that time Jesus began to show to His disciples that He must go to Jerusalem, and suffer many things from the elders and chief priests and scribes, and be killed, and be raised the third day. 22<u>Then Peter took Him aside and began to rebuke Him, saying, "Far be it from You, Lord; this shall not happen to You!"</u> 23But He turned and said to Peter, "Get behind Me, Satan! You are an offense to

153

Me, for you are not mindful of the things of God but the things of men.'' (Matthew 16:21-23 NKJV)

Through the gift of the discerning spirits, our Lord Jesus Christ saw beyond Peter and saw Satan instead; He rebuked Satan firmly!

Another example was Apostle Paul's ability to discern an evil spirit behind a young girl proclaiming a goodwill message after them in Antioch's city. He saw that she was operating with a demonic spirit, and he rebuked the evil spirit and cast it out.

[16]'Now it happened as we went to prayer, that a certain slave girl possessed with a spirit of divination met us, who brought her masters much profit by fortune-telling. [17]This girl followed Paul and us, and cried out, saying, ''These men are the servants of the Most High God, who proclaim to us the way of salvation.'' [18]And this she did for many days. But Paul, greatly annoyed, turned and said to the spirit, ''I command you in the name of Jesus Christ to come out of her.'' And he came out that very hour.' (Acts 16:16-18 NKJV)

In the Mercies of God, this gift, the Discerning of Spirits, among others, operates in my life and ministry. It is this gift of the discerning of spirits that granted me insight into this particular principality. I call it 'The Marital Monster'. For its manifestation is nothing short of a monster.

The gift of the discerning of spirit is common among those God granted to operate in the Prophetic's office; this gift enables one to see clearly into the Spirit realm, understanding the operations of the spirit, particularly seeing angels or demons at work per time. In the Mercies of GOD, This gift is operating powerfully in my life and ministry.

As a Life Coach and an Intercessor, I see deeply into people, nations, and persons' issues and circumstances; I do not invoke this gift myself; as the Spirit wills, He grants me insights from time to time.

This Gift also works hand in hand with the Gifts of The Word of Knowledge and the Word of Wisdom, where a deep understanding of issues are revealed and divine way out granted, respectively.

Brother Kenneth E. Hagin, in His book 'The Holy Spirit and His Gifts', elaborated extensively on these different gifts and their operations. His books are a Blessing, highly recommended; please endeavour to read them!

The Spirit of God opened my eyes to this evil spirit I call 'The Marital Monster.' Below are some of its striking characteristics:

- They operate in marriages where both partners are not in tune with the Holy Spirit. Most of the time, One spouse is compromised, either as an unbeliever, carnal man, or a believer, with a non-submissive mind to Christ.

155

- This marital monster operates only to attack the salvation and faith of the partner that is inclined to submit to God's will.

- This demon takes advantage of the influence in marriage and high-jack the unwilling partner's mind to negatively influence and oppose the willing partner.

- This evil spirit can possess a male or a female. As long the person is receptive to a compromised mind, the evil spirit will possess them.

> *They made the possessed impossible, unresponsive, unwilling to cooperate, very difficult and very beastly, in short, turning the possessed partner into a 'monster'.*

- They target partners that seek God and willing to do the will of God in marriage to torture and distract such from their faith.

- They made the possessed impossible, unresponsive, unwilling to cooperate, very difficult and very beastly, in short, turning the possessed partner into a 'monster'.

- The possessed partner may not be fully aware of this oppression. However, they would have accommodated an un-submissive mind, carnality and unwillingness to submit to the will of God, even if they were ministers of the Gospel.

- Marital Monster's target is not only to the possessed but also to the other partner.

- The Marital Monster also hides under the inferiority complex of a partner to buffet the other. Often, the oppressed one has an underlining inferiority complex against their partner's giftings.

- The possessed 'marital monster' partner exhibits pseudo-sound morality as a deception; however, watching keenly, there are clear cut sins in their lives as typical of all demons and force of darkness!

- The oppressed often do not submit to reasoning nor Godly counsel. No matter what you do to them, they will not budge. They usually do not have respect nor regard for divine authority!

- Due to the challenging and beastly behaviour of the possessed partner, the other partner is subjected to a miserable life. The possessed one could be a man or a woman. It does not matter.

- This attack causes the willing partner much pain, facing between obeying God and a problematic partner. If a man, the 'monster wife' could become so wayward, abusive, and oppressing, ridiculing the husband, who many a time may be pastor, a leader in the church, or a respected man in the society.

This reproach will become a source of embarrassment and reproach to him. No matter what the man does, the 'marital monster' possessed woman will stop at nothing to ridicule her husband, deny him intimacy, and push him into adultery until

157

eventually, the man commits suicide. He loses his job, ministry, faith, and all. We rebuke such evil in the Name of YESHUA HAMASHIACH (JESUS CHRIST), Amen.

- In the case of a woman, the 'marital monster' possessed man can become so complicated, non-responsive, wayward, yet not allowing the woman freedom. Some of such evil possessed men become highly abusive, hitting the woman regularly, even as ministers of the Gospel. The woman as the victim may be abandoned, left to care alone for their children, denied intimacy. The monster-possessed man could keep the woman in malice for many years. We judge this evil in the Name of YESHUA HAMASHIACH (JESUS CHRIST), Amen.

- This principality is not just a demon that can be easily cast out. Because of their operation's peculiarity, they carry with them, subjecting their partners to the baggage of emotional torture, pain, denial, reproach, and temptations.

Eventually, the marital monster will also cause the oppressed to commit suicide, self-destruction and guilt-laden, for the enormity of evil they had caused their spouses. As the Bible says, *'The thief comes not but to steal, to kill, and to destroy.'* This evil spirit eventually destroys the oppressed if there is no divine intervention to stop the course of things.

I see this evil spirit again and again.

What is very surprising to me is the very striking characteristics in all and every circumstance. I could almost finish the story for the victims when they are narrating their ordeal. Very precise, because it is the same evil spirit, targeting Godly marriages!

Can you relate to the above characteristics in some marital crises you see around you? This evil spirit is real, tormenting several homes today, rendering the beloved of God oppressed, emotionally tortured and abused. Many had become victims of mental oppression because of this evil force.

OVERCOMING THE MARITAL MONSTER.
- Identify the Marital Monster.

The evil spirit, Marital Monster, is not in operation in every home or marital crisis. This evil force is specific, peculiar, and has definite characteristics and striking features that you will know in manifestation.

Many called such a person difficult; however, this evil force is a demonic force targeting the other partner. The oppressed often do not submit to reasoning nor Godly counsel.

Does the above description fit your difficult partner or spouse? Do they exhibit and manifest some or all of the above traits? It does not matter if they are in church or not; they are somehow compromised in their mind towards God, hence opening the door for this evil spirit to possess and use them as a vessel to buffet you especially.

Similarly, do you fit the descriptions expressed above? Do you see yourself acting beyond your control in a manner that looks like a monster towards your spouse?.

Acknowledging the presence of this evil demon is key to overcoming them. The enemy deceives many into thinking and saying it is the other person's fault; they also suggest you try some character adjustments or go for another person. However, the main target is to attack and torture your faith and salvation in Christ.

- Recognise that it is a spiritual battle, not a character or emotional battle.

Many tackle this physically, leading them into deeper frustrations. Many begged and begged the possessed spouse, to no avail. Many tried to do everything to appease the evil spirit, only to enter deeper frustrations.

The attack is demonic; hence, begging or other physical attempts will never solve it. The demon must be rebuked and cast off the marriage. That is the way to go. However, just praying it once may not yield the desired answer because of the attached emotional connectivity.

It is essential to take your eyes off your spouse. The attack is beyond them; it is not just them hating you; the devil takes over their lives to buffet you through their compromised life.

- Take a step of faith.

Enquire of the Lord, what is the anchor this evil spirit is hanging onto in your life. For the enemy to attack anyone, he must have an anchor to hold. Such anchor could be sin (self-acquired or inherited sins), disobedience, unbelief, bitterness, unforgiveness, or ignorance. These anchors differ from one person to another.

Identifying the actual anchor is why the Prayer of Enquiry is vital; asking God, Why is this? What is the source of this attack? You are to ask in the Name of Jesus Christ, expecting God to answer you in His time.

If you genuinely ask God for the anchor the enemy is hanging onto in your life, He will tell you. Once you understand what this evil force is hanging onto in your life, take necessary actions; if they are due to sins, repent; if disobedience, repents and take action. As you cut off this anchor, rebuking the evil force becomes easy.

-Take with you Word.

Stand on the word of God for your marriage, and begin to war with the word. Insist on the deliverance you have in Christ Jesus and the authority we inherit in Christ Jesus. Begin to battle with these.

Things may not turn around overnight; however, they will eventually, if you stay in faith. This attack focuses on emotional and familiar connectivity; hence, taking a step of faith can be clouded with the emotions and character traits of the possessed one. **You easily tilt towards being angry with them, wondering why they cannot reason with you. All of these, standing as a barrier to the walk of faith. Do not allow this barrier to distract you!**

This barrier is why you must engage the Word long enough until all doubts and distractions are taken out of the way, and the Word of God prevails and becomes your reality.

- Rebuke the marital monster.

Eventually, you have to rebuke the marital monster. Rebuking them is how they will bow and leave your marriage. However, engaging the above steps are critical to effective rebuking and casting out this evil spirit.

- Walk in love.

In the fight against this evil spirit, the marital monster will demand walking in love. As explained above, the possessed spouse will become so difficult, beastly and mean, you will be tempted to fight back. You will prefer not to have anything to do with them. You may also be tempted to nurture bitterness, resentment and accommodate unforgiveness against your spouse.

This scenario is the case in many homes where the couple still lives together despite the evil spirit. The attacked one will become embittered and unforgiving. This bitterness is an additional open door for the enemy, leading to more oppression and evil.

These side attacks are why walking in Love is crucial in overcoming this evil force called 'the marital monster'. You have to make up your mind to walk in love, no matter what. Distance yourself, if need be, if the spouse is physically abusive; however, choose to forgive, stand on walking in love, so you do not give the devil further opportunities to buffet your home.

- Seek Help

Because of the peculiarity of this attack, victims of marital crises should seek expert helps. There are many professional marriage counsellors and experts in this area of life. There are many laws in place for these kinds of cases.

Please endeavour to seek help accordingly. In addition to scientific and expert supports, please, focus on engaging God in this case. We pray God to heal your marriage in the Name of YESHUA HAMASHIACH (JESUS CHRIST), Amen.

We run a LIFE Coaching, an online faith-based Life coaching programme, setting men up with God for a Glorious Turnaround. It is a specialized online retreat targeting specific needs and a do-it-yourself goal meeting deliverance and solution hub. If you are willing to participate or receive further support in this area, do not hesitate to contact us via Email: info@air.church

We pray for you today; if you are a victim of this evil force, the 'marital monster', we judge the evil spirit and break its hold over your life and destiny. We remove every anchor they are holding on to by the Blood of Jesus. We declare that you are FREE in the Name of Jesus Christ, Amen.

WHAT OF CHRISTIANS THAT SEEK DIVORCE.

Every Marriage is a Miracle! There is no Christian marriage that is not mendable, none. No one. Because the 3rd Person in marriage, when acknowledged and referenced, He makes a customized escape for all crisis.

The question for the Christian couples involved is: are you Christians? Are you yielding or willing to submit to the Spirit of GOD in you?

When the Spirit of God nudged us to take on this Book series, I was exceedingly reluctant because this was where I failed the most; Marriage, I thought!

However, as we began to dig into this, seeing the different reasons marriages work and why they do not, starting from understanding marriage to the preparations for marriage to the choosing for marriage, the compatibilities, the multiplications, and the reigning stages. Marital outcomes become more apparent to me!

'For with God, nothing shall be impossible.' (Luke 1:37 NKJV).

'Jesus said to him, "if you can believe, all things are possible to him who believes." (Mark 9:23 NKJV)

When asked about divorce in the Bible, Our Lord Jesus Christ says:

³'The Pharisees also came to Him, testing Him, and saying to Him, "Is it lawful for a man to divorce his wife for just any reason?" ⁴And He answered and said to them, "Have you not read that He who made them at the beginning 'made them male and female,' ⁵and said, 'For this reason a man shall leave his father and mother and be joined to his wife, and the two shall become one flesh'? ⁶So then, they are no longer two but one flesh. Therefore what God has joined together, let no man separate." (Matthew 19:3-6 NKJV)

> **Proper troubleshooting of the cause of the crisis in a marriage, addressing them accordingly, choosing to align with the 3ʳᵈ Person in Marriage can and will remedy and heal any marital crisis.**

Nevertheless, just like everything in life, life's outcome is based on the choices made and the willingness to choose God in one's affairs or not. Hence, choosing divine intervention in your marriage will entirely be up to you!

Our GOD is good, and His mercies endure forevermore, Amen.

Your Notes . . .

The Marital Monster. Can you identify some of its striking characteristics?

Your Notes . . .

How can one overcome this evil force in our lives and that of our loved ones?

The 3rd Person in Marriage

....BEING SINGLE

9. ···BEING SINGLE

... BEING SINGLE

This chapter focuses on some exceptional cases of being single. Not the unmarried teenagers or the young adults; these are single due to age, and it's simply a phase and a stage in life development.

The single ones we address here are those singles due to a long time waiting for suitors without success, also the singles who used to be married or married briefly and got out of the marriage within two years of marriage.

Others to be addressed are those married for a long time, without kids, divorced or separated for good. Others are single because their marital crisis is simply unbearable, or the spouse ran away, or the spouse became gay, the spouse became abusive and dangerous, the spouse simply not responding. Still, some are those single with children, either as baby mamas, officially divorced, side chicks with benefits that turned into baby mamas, and finally, those single due to their spouses' death.

These sets of singles are seen in both men and women. Many men are single due to abusive wives, troubled marriages, or their wives running away with other men. Others are single due to a lack of courage to approach a woman, hiding away under career for years. Some are single due to the loss of a spouse and left to care for the children alone.

The list is on and on. In the mercies of God, we will be delving into some truth on being single. Irrespective of your degree of brokenness or wholeness, the 3rd person in Marriage cares and has provision for all. Let us dig into this...

SOME CAUSES OF BEING SINGLE.
I. BEING SINGLE DUE TO LACK OF SUITORS.

As casual and straightforward as this may look, many people fall into this category. They are single simply because no one is coming for their hands in marriage, or as a man, due to lack of will or courage to approach women. The few ones they attempted did not succeed, hence losing all courage to try again.

There are two sides to this category. Spiritual and Physical. In dealing with this kind of singleness, such a person is encouraged to take up the battle first spiritually. This case should be addressed as oppression and taken authority over every stagnation and delay in the Name of CHRIST JESUS.

As the spiritual intervention goes on, it is also very important to address the physical aspect. Engaging supports from loved ones, attempting services such as dating sites, if no loved one can take on this, will go a long way to help.

Many churches organize singles forums; however, attending and participating in such meetings becomes a reproach when someone has been single for a long time, especially if the organizers are not skilful to cater to these mature singles.

Many independent marriage ministries are in the Church today, so also are social dating sites. If the situations are addressed spiritually, to negate oppression, engaging these other options will birth success. Many great relationships are born from these dating services. There is someone for you around you, and we pray that the Mercies of God prevail for you to be connected to your mate in the Name of YESHUA HAMASHIACH (JESUS CHRIST), Amen.

II. BEING SINGLE BY CHOICE.

Many today decided to remain single; when you ask them, they would first say, it's a choice, 'I love being single.' Today such people are being celebrated. However, delving deeper into their lives' history, such decisions may be revealed to be born from past pain, abusive background, disappointments, or fear of the unknown, having seen many that had been in pain around them.

With the world of civilization, educations, and freedom to earn a living for all, it becomes easy for such persons to live a seemingly 'fulfilled life,' as they can carry out most of the life endeavours, vocations, pleasures, vacations as a single person. Today, Self-centeredness is being promoted on a large scale. However, exploring deep always revealed unsatisfied life!

It was not until the Spirit of God revealed to me when we were taking on a series titled 'Unveiling the faces of the Anti-Christ' that we saw how oppressing and deceptive self-centeredness is. Having been through a series of trials and oppressions, the enemy always lurks around his victims to promote self-centeredness, self-sufficiency, 'self-love', 'Me, myself and I'. all of these are a plot to erect the mountain of self against God. They are staging man independent of God while disguising as their lord. No man is independent, you are either submissive to God, or you are to Satan.

When a man claims he is independent of God, such a one is being fooled and deceived by the enemy. Although he may not reference God, he is submissive to another, which is Satan, the spirit that rules in the lives of the disobediences and lawless persons.

'And you He made alive, who were dead in trespasses and sins, [2]in which you once walked according to the course of this world, according to the prince of the power of the air, the spirit who now works in the sons of disobedience,

³Among whom also we all once conducted ourselves in the lusts of our flesh, fulfilling the desires of the flesh and of the mind, and were by nature children of wrath, just as the others.' (Ephesians 2:1-3 NKJV)

Man created in the image and likeness of God can be independent and alienated from God if care is not taken. This ability is why, in creating man, God ensuring the spiritual aspect is expected to be occupied by Him while with the soulish realm (will, mind, and emotions) and physical senses, man could relate and operate with others and function on this earth.

Proper troubleshooting of the cause of the crisis in a marriage, addressing them accordingly, choosing to align with the 3rd Person in Marriage can and will remedy and heal any marriage crisis.

No man is independent; every man is an outcome of their spiritual dispositions. It is important because the enemy deceives many to think they are independent while indirectly ruling them to manipulate them.

You can see details of 'some steps to overcoming self-centeredness in our new book 'The Spirit Realm.'

The Bible says that woo to him who is single in the days of adversity! Explaining that two are better than one, that it is not good for man to be alone, and so on.

Being single is not the perfect will of God for any man. Irrespective of your vocation or achievements in life and ministry, being single is not the perfect will of God for you. The mandate upon every man is to be 'Fruitful, Multiply, Fill the earth, Subdue, and have Dominion'. (Genesis 1:28)

God gave man the honour of choices in life, and only what you choose is permitted to happen to you. Therefore, no one can do anything about this when men are cajoled or coaxed by the enemy to decide to remain single in life. Until you are willing, you will not eat the good of the land.

Irrespective of the degree of wholeness or brokenness, if you do not conclude that you will remain single, you will not be single. However, if you concede to being single due to pressure, abuse, or the fear of the unknown, as a man thinks in himself, so is he.

Therefore, we are encouraged to have an open mind, choose to live the real, fulfilled life God created for us. Trust God for a miracle, choose to live the best of you in this world, trust God, and leave the 'HOW' to God. Be fruitful, multiply, fill the earth, subdue and have dominion over all oppositions to your fruitfulness.

Give that tiny window of opportunity to God for a miracle, irrespectively of the degree of your brokenness or wholeness. God will show up for you.

'For with God, nothing will be impossible.' (Luke 1:37 NKJV)

Nevertheless, please let it not be due to any form of oppression from the enemy if you wish to remain single. Shalom.

III. BEING SINGLE DUE TO OPPRESSION.

Many people today are single due to circumstances beyond them. Many people were highly abused in their marriages, that the safest harbour was to remain single. Many also are single today because they cannot fathom why; they have prayed, attended deliverance services, and fast, given to churches, yet, the circumstances did not change. The oppression sometimes could be so real that they know their cases are not ordinary!

Many tend to deal with oppression-based singleness as solely physical, character relating or compatibility issues in this circumstance. In our earlier chapter, we introduced the Marital Monster; A demonic oppression that takes advantage of a spouse's openness to be used by the devil, hijacking them and setting them up to torture and torment the other spouse— literally acting like a monster in the marriage. Many people become single due to this evil force.

We dealt a bit on this principality; they are not the lowest-ranked fallen angels; they are middle-ranked, operating at influential gates to buffet the other spouse. This principality is the force responsible for many abusive marriages.

It is safe to take cover in light of the abuse and physical torment in a relationship and seek professional marriage counsellors and expert interventions.

In addition, being single due to oppression is encouraged to be addressed spiritually, as the evil forces can be rebuked and overcome, and peace can reign in the family again. The 3rd Person in Marriage can foster a miraculous way out for anyone who aligns with Him in this circumstance. We will look into how to overcome such in the next chapter.

The key highlight here is that our Lord Jesus Christ had fully paid for all oppressions; hence, this evil force can be overturned and rebuked in every circumstance. However, the willingness to take on the journey of deliverance is key to its attainment.

IV. BEING SINGLE DUE TO THE ABSENCE OF SPOUSE.

As we were wrapping this chapter up, the Spirit of God nudged me to add this category; singleness due to the spouse's absence. Many today have very sick or very ill spouses, some with mental difficulties, others in a critical or vegetable state, hence non-responding.

Some with missing spouses, and no one knows their whereabouts for a very long time. These people may not be dead; however, they can no longer perform and occupy their roles as husband or wife, companion, lovers, friends, and all.

The spouses of these ill or sick persons, saddled with not just the burden of taking care of them; they are also made 'single' technically. This state of being single may be temporal and sometimes for a very long time. They had to make all the decisions by themselves, yet without the comforting company of their lovers.

Many people fall into this category. If that is you, we pray that the Mercy of GOD prevails for you in the Name of YESHUA HAMASHIACH (JESUS CHRIST), Amen. This category is worsened because many such singles are suffering yet cannot come out of such relationships.

A miracle is what such a one needs, and a MIRACLE, a customised miracle, is what you will get in the Name of YESHUA HAMASHIACH (JESUS CHRIST), Amen.

Turn the burden unto Jesus, cast your burden unto Him, and you will be surprised how He will sort you out. We pray for a customized miracle for you today, in the Name of Yeshua Hamashiach (Jesus Christ), Amen.

V. BEING SINGLE DUE TO A NATURAL LOSS.

Many are single today due to the loss of their loved ones, so sorry about that. It is becoming a common occurrence in our world today. It is not the perfect will of God for anyone, irrespective of the circumstances surrounding the death. Many are dying today untimely due to a lack of understanding of spirituality, unbelief, disobedience or sins. As much as these are the fact, losing a loved one is not desirous in any way.

The Bible encourages re-marrying, especially if the widow or the widower is young and under 60 years because it is not God's will to be single!

Many people in this situation simply cannot pass the pain, the attachment, and the intimacy they shared with their deceased loved ones. Many of such are soulmates and could hardly trust another person intimately. The devil is a liar! We rebuke the devil in the Name of YESHUA HAMASHIACH (Jesus Christ), Amen.

Like we discussed earlier, as long as you are open to God and do not invoke your will to remain single, God can and will sort you out miraculously. He specialises in impossibilities. *'For with God, nothing shall be impossible.'* (Luke 1:37 NKJV). God has done this for many and can still sort you out, even with your pieces of baggage: old age, children, lovelessness, etc.

Let God, and He will sort you out in a most miraculous way. Remember, He loves you indeed, and even though it was not His perfect will to see you in this state, He can make good of your circumstances and turn it around for your good indeed. We pray you find your peace in the Name of YESHUA HAMASHIACH (JESUS CHRIST), Amen.

HEALING FOR THE SINGLES.

Having looked into some case studies and causes for being single, we hope your case or that of your loved one is covered in the above. There may be more causes; however, It is now time to see how to receive healing from being single. As you endeavour to take these steps, we pray that you will encounter the 3rd Person in Marriage, who will work a customized miracle for you, or your loved ones, in the name of YESHUA HAMASHIACH (JESUS CHRIST), Amen.

I. ENGAGE GOD.

First thing first, check your alignment with God. How much of God do you manifest? It has nothing to do with how long you stay in church or how many church activities you engage in weekly. You may be a titled leader in the church yet be so distant from God. It is prioritizing your relationship with God that matters, rightly engaging God.

> *As you increase your knowledge of God, your authority to overcome life circumstances will increase, and more wins experienced.*

Personal communion with the Father is key to all victories in life. As much as it is essential to be associated with a local assembly, it is also very good to access the Anointing available in the Fuller Church (The body of Christ). If you know that your relationship with God has not been great, check in to a faith believing church or ministry organizing retreats, conferences, or seminars. Build up your faith, listen to tapes of great men of God, attend workshops on faith, not necessarily on marriage.

Take a break from the marriage trouble, focus on knowing God more. As you increase your knowledge of God, your authority to overcome life circumstances will increase, and more wins experienced.

It is your call. Search for conferences and seminars, ask from persons who are sound in the Lord; sometimes, it may be books that you need to read to encounter revival.

Meanwhile, in our ministry, The Church in the air, we run a LIFE Coaching, an online retreat program, setting men up with God for a Glorious Turnaround. It is a do-it-yourself, self-paced, mobile-friendly, yet Life impacting online retreat tailored to specific needs. You get to set your desired goals and watch them come to pass. You may want to check this out if you need this or know someone that needs this. www.coaching.air.church is the link to the platform. You can send an email for more information to info@air.church

This step, Engaging God, is placed as the first step for a reason. When you align yourself with God, every other thing will follow. Therefore, go on the journey of aligning yourself with God. Learn more about God. Tell God, 'I want to know you more,' and if you are sincere, He will lead you aright to the right place and right people to build up your faith.

Remember that most of the problems that men face are ignorance-based problems. As you increase your knowledge of God, your faith is built, and your capacity to overcome problems increases. Let us see the other steps after this...

II. BE HAPPY.

After aligning with God, the second step in tackling being single is choosing to be happy. Singleness birth a lot of depression, especially when you see your siblings, friends, colleagues and neighbours flaunting their seemingly 'successful marriages' before you. Even if it were not intentional, the enemy would always remind you that you are missing such unions.

> *No one can fake unhappiness; if you are not happy, it will show eventually.*

Because of these, many people become isolated, withdrawing from social gatherings and not mingling with others. Trying to cope on your own will not be fruitful. This is why, as a single one, it is time to align yourself with the higher purpose that can bring happiness your way, irrespective of the reason for being single.

No one can fake unhappiness; if you are not happy, it will show eventually. Therefore, sit down, access your career, vocations, interests, dreams, abilities, skills, and gifts. What area can you lash on to bring in some more success? Success brings happiness; get some success in other areas of your life. Learn a new trade, start a new business, improve yourself, get some extra degrees, make some more money. As the cash rolls in, smiles will also roll in.

This step is crucial because what the enemy wants is unhappy to buffet you the more. Give him no such leisure. Create other successes around you. Remember, the mandate of God upon your life is to be 'Fruitful, Multiply, Fill the earth, Subdue and have Dominion.' Insist on being fruitful and becoming successful. These successes also attract more success, including marital breakthroughs.

Be happy, create success, be fruitful, and more shall be given unto him that has this.

'For whoever has, to him more will be given; but whoever does not have, even what he has will be taken away from him.' (Mark 4:25 NKJV)

When you are happy and create more happiness and success, even more of such will be given unto you. Your happiness is attracting many good things to you daily. Amen!

Pause, ponder and think about this!

III. BE ATTRACTIVE.

Marriage is both physical and spiritual. Marriage involves physical intimacy. Marriage involves liking a physical man or a physical woman. Therefore, it is important to bring out your 'A game', your best shot, in your physical presentation.

Boost your looks. Sharp it up; the whole world is focusing on looks today, the competition is intense. Therefore, a not-ready, *'I-don't-care'* looking person will have no place in the race. *'My spouse will like me the way I am'* will not work today. Do not be the way you are, be the best you can ever be. Go extra! **Beauty is embedded inside everyone. Bring out your beauty!**

Oh, I do not have time, I do not know how to, I do not like make-up, this is just me. All of those will not work. Break off these relationship myths. Go extra. Spice up your wardrobe and get new shoes and new looks; applicable for males and females.

Especially the male, clean up! For both, get into the gym, get into the stores, and spice things up. There are many Do-it-yourself self-help videos on YouTube and other social media; check them out and bring out your best for your God's best.

As you make yourself more attractive, every other thing, being equal, you are on your way to your desired answers. Being good looking will be a decision and a choice to make. Make that choice, Bring out you're A-game, Bless the world with your BEST!

IV. ABSTAIN FROM SINS.

Long-standing problems are notorious for attracting sins. Such common sins are Doubts, Unbeliefs, Bitterness against God, Sexual sins, Unforgiveness, Bitterness against some persons, etc. In this case, Sexual immoralities are common with single persons. The enemy lurks around to suggest casual sexual pleasures and immoralities to make up for the loneliness. And as you embrace these sins, many of which could be very private, the immediate gratification blinds the mind to the fact that the enemy now has more legal access into your life, thus elongating the oppressions and adding some more afflictions!

> *And as you embrace these sins, many of which could be very private, the immediate gratification blinds the mind to the fact that the enemy now has more legal access into your life, thus elongating the oppressions and adding some more.*

It is why many people with long-standing issues also come up with unexplainable sicknesses, afflictions, lack and unrelating pains. Sins are a sure entrance of the devil into anyone's life, irrespective of who you are, be it a pastor or a church member.

What then is the way out? How can one be sane, stable, and normal as a single without sexual pleasure and satisfaction?

Well, the good news is, there is a way of escape for believers in Grace. God factors in Grace to help those in critical needs. In our book: *[10]Understanding the works of darkness,'* we dealt extensively with Sins Dynamics; you may want to lay hold on a copy, so you may know how to break yourself off sins that easily beset believers that are in long-standing problems.

Let us take a very close look at this all-liberating scripture. The details can be accessed in the mentioned book above.

[15]'For we do not have a High Priest who cannot sympathize with our weaknesses, but was in all points tempted as we are, yet without sin. [16]Let us therefore come boldly to the throne of grace, that we may obtain mercy and find grace to help you in time of need.' (Hebrews 4:15-16 NKJV)

Take a second look at the scriptures above and let us analyse them as follows:

- **Your High Priest sympathizes with you**. He understands your circumstances and your need for sexual satisfaction. He knows you need that intimacy and that pleasure.

- **Our Lord Jesus Christ, your High Priest, had been tempted at all instances, yet without sin, so it is possible to be without sin in any situation.**

---

[10] Understanding the works of darkness by pst tomowo on amazon

A quick one here, you may ask. How was Jesus tempted as I am? was He married, divorced, or denied a relationship? In the formation of sin, the thoughts come first, then the conception of the thoughts, then the manifestation of the sins, then the addiction or deadness by the sin.

[14]*'But each one is tempted when he is drawn away by his own desires and enticed. [15]Then, when desire has conceived, it gives birth to sin; and sin, when it is full-grown, brings forth death.'* *(James 1:14-15 NKJV)*

> *Any sin that you allow in your thoughts will manifest in due time. Good news, any wrong you overcome at your thought level, you will never commit! It was how our Lord Jesus Christ prevailed over all sins! He did not allow them in His thoughts!*

Therefore, before you ever fall into that sin, you thought of it and conceived it.

Consequently, you have already failed at your thought level, where sins are conceived and charged against one.

Any sin that you allow in your thoughts will manifest in due time. Good news, any wrong you overcome at your thought level, you will never commit! It was how our Lord Jesus Christ prevailed over all sins! He did not allow them in His thoughts; hence He overcame them all and could not manifest them for real.

(You can see more details about this in our book 'Understanding the works of darkness.'

- He, therefore, charged that you come boldly for help. Coming boldly, not proudly. Boldly because you will be helped. Not proudly because He is not approving sins, as the solution cost Him much -His life!

- Come boldly to the Throne of Grace. The place is called the Throne of Grace. Because Grace is what is dispensed there. What is Grace; it is the unmerited ability of God in Man.

- To obtain Mercy. The password to this all-liberating Throne of Grace is MERCY. When you go to God for mercy, you are invariably accessing the Throne of Grace.

- And you will find Grace to help in time of need. As you enter the Throne of Grace with your password, Mercy, Grace will be dispensed unto you.

Summarily, as you ask God sincerely for Mercy over any sin committed, you are engaging your password to enter the Throne of Grace. Just before you leave, Grace is poured unto you. If you repeat this again and again, soon, you will discover that you have overcome the sin.

This secret is vital; please keep it well. Many people do not enjoy this because they take God's Mercy for granted; they forget to say,

'Am sorry.' Hence, they expose themselves to the enemy that elongates their oppression and misses out on the Grace to help them.

My dear friend, what will you rather do with this information? Many people today are in elongated oppression because of the associated sins they incurred along the way. They wonder why God is not answering them for many years, not knowing that they have granted the enemy legal access through 'side-sins.' He that has an ear let him hear what the Spirit says to the churches.

As you ask God sincerely for Mercy over any sin committed, you are engaging your password to enter the Throne of Grace. Just before you leave, Grace is poured unto you. If you repeat this again and again, soon, you will discover that you have overcome the sin.

V. REBUKE THE DEVIL.

In overcoming all life issues, including this issue of being single, and especially all the long-standing problems, the place of demonic interference can never be overlooked. Demonic influences are powering most long-standing oppressions; this is why there is a need to take authority over them. Our Lord Jesus Christ, as He was rounding up here on earth, said:

¹⁸'And Jesus came and spoke to them, saying, "<u>All authority has been given to Me in heaven and on earth.</u> ¹⁹Go therefore and make disciples of all the nations, baptizing them in the name of the Father and of the Son and of the Holy Spirit, ²⁰teaching them to observe all things that I have commanded you; <u>and lo, I am with you always, even to the end of the age.</u>" Amen. (Matthew 28:18-20 NKJV)

¹⁵'And He said to them, "Go into all the world and preach the gospel to every creature. ¹⁶He who believes and is baptized will be saved; but he who does not believe will be condemned. ¹⁷<u>And these signs will follow those who believe: In My Name they will cast out demons;</u> they will speak with new tongues; ¹⁸they will take up serpents; and if they drink anything deadly, it will by no means hurt them; they will lay hands on the sick, and they will recover.' (Mark 16:16-18 NKJV)

¹⁸'And He said to them, "I saw Satan fall like lightning from heaven. ¹⁹<u>Behold, I give you authority to trample on serpents and scorpions, and over all the power of the enemy, and nothing shall by any means hurt you.</u> ²⁰Nevertheless do not rejoice in this, that the spirits are subject to you, but rather rejoice because your names are written in heaven (Luke 10:18-20 NKJV)

From the above three scriptures, it was evident that our Lord Jesus Christ had given the believers, you and I, the power of attorney to use His Name.

We have the authority over all forces of darkness. We have the authority to cast out demons; we have the authority to be whatever God has called us to be, to have what God has given us, and to do what God has asked us to do.

I speak this into myself every day, and I see myself taking charge of all forces of darkness. You can join me as follows:

All authority is given to our Lord JESUS CHRIST, in heaven and earth. By faith, I have this Authority. I have Authority to Be, I have Authority to Have, and I have Authority to Do.

> **All authority is given to our Lord JESUS CHRIST, in heaven and earth.**
>
> **By faith, I have this Authority.**
> **I have Authority to Be,**
> **I have Authority to Have,**
> **and I have Authority to Do.**

Say this again and again; you have the power of attorney to use the Name of Jesus Christ.

Rebuke the devil, tagged him with the situation; You spirit of delay, the spirit of singleness, barrenness, the spirit of oppression. I rebuke you in the Name of JESUS CHRIST, Amen.

Tag them as they present, and use your authority in Christ. At first, they may seem non-responding, insist, insist that you have authority over them, and say it again and again until your circumstances changes. They must because all of them must bow to the Name of JESUS CHRIST, Amen.

I pray that the Name of Jesus Christ begins to work for you in the Name of Jesus Christ, Amen.

Affirm this in your life daily.

All authority is given to our Lord JESUS CHRIST, in heaven and earth. By faith, I have this Authority. I have Authority to Be, I have Authority to Have, and I have Authority to Do.

As you declare this and do not stop, the Word you are speaking will become your reality!

VI. GIVE GOD A CHANCE.

Finally, in the journey of healing being single, it is very important to give God a chance to work a customized miracle for you. As your case is peculiar, so will be your miracle. There is a way out of your situation; there is a way of escape. How God will work it out in your case may differ from other persons with a seemingly similar situation. Allow God, Give God a chance, Tell Him to do His perfect work in you. Then, trust Him as the Holy Spirit begin to lead you in what to do.

Some suggestions may seem ridiculous; some may look or sound very simple and unbelievably easy to accomplish, as you have handed over your case to God, casting all your care unto Him. He will step in and begin to intervene.

When those ideas, suggestions and inner witnesses (as we explained in an earlier chapter) come your way, trust them and take corresponding actions.

'Casting all your care upon Him, for He cares for you.' (1 Peter 5:7 NKJV)

In every miracle creation, there is a part of God and a part of man. God will do the supernatural, while man will do the natural.

> **In every miracle creation, there is a part of God and a part of man. God will do the supernatural, while man will do the natural.**

As you journey to your miracle, The Holy Spirit will prompt you into taking some actions such as start this new course, change your wardrobe, stop this habit, start this outreach, visit that family, etc. I do not know what He will tell you to do, as they will be tailored to your case and easily accessible and doable for you!

Once you hear God tell you to do something and confirm with the Holy Spirit's inner witness, take action, be bold about it, and you will return with your testimonies. I pray that you will encounter your desired miracles in the Name of YESHUA HAMASHIACH (JESUS CHRIST), Amen.

It is not the perfect will of God to be single and to remain single. If you so desire, ask God today, take the suggested steps above, and The Way, Himself (JESUS CHRIST), will make a WAY for you.

'Jesus said to him, "I am the way, the truth, and the life. No one comes to the Father except through Me.' (John 14:6 NKJV)

Nevertheless, remember that *'The abilities of good are of God. The abilities of evil are of darkness; however, the will to make a choice is of man. When a man makes a choice, the corresponding abilities back him. Now, man will be responsible for the choices he makes today and on the day of judgement.'* So, choose wisely. Shalom.

VII. RETURN TO GIVE GOD THANKS.

BE GRATEFUL. In your journey to your desired miracle, God will throw some small wins at you, small miracles, small breakthroughs. They are for a purpose; as you reference and acknowledge these miracles, more shall be given unto you, until one day, you look, and you are already in your complete miracle!

Many, not understanding the scriptures, ignore these Divine strategies. They become beclouded with the main prayer points and do not see nor grateful for the little other things God is already doing in their lives. They thereby miss out on the major miracle as a result. Let us see how the word of God addresses this:

'For whoever has, to him more will be given; but whoever does not have, even what he has will be taken away from him.' (Mark 4:25 NKJV)

One day the Spirit of God opened my eyes to see that this scripture was repeated five times in the Gospel. (Matthew 13:12; Matthew 25:29; Mark 4:25; Luke 8:18; and Luke 19:26). This repetition could not be a coincidence. Pay attention to this. If you have, more will be given to you; if you do not have, even what you have will be taken from you. Think about this. In the journey to creating your miracle, Gratitude and thanksgiving for the little new things GOD is doing will lead to your seeing more and more of such wins until you are in your miracle!

Our Lord JESUS CHRIST brought this point out clearly when He healed ten lepers in Luke 17: He started the healing and sent them to the priest for cleansing. On their way, however, when one of them discovered that he was healed, he returned to give God thanks and received the complete package of his miracle. He became whole. Our Lord Jesus asked, Were there not ten cleansed, where are the remaining nine? Why was He asking? **Because being grateful for the little is the pathway to your wholeness!**

17'And Jesus answering said, Were there not ten cleansed? but where are the nine? 18There are not found that returned to give glory to God, save this stranger. 19And He said unto him, 'Arise, go thy way: thy faith hath made thee whole.' (Luke 17:17-19 KJV)

195

When you return to give God thanks for the little ones you are seeing, you receive the complete package of your miracle!

Therefore, as you journey to your marital breakthrough, watch out for the little new things God is doing in your life and give Him thanks for them.

'For whoever has, to him more will be given; but whoever does not have, even what he has will be taken away from him.' (Mark 4:25 NKJV)

This point will bring us to the final chapter of this book. Managing crisis of Choosing in Marriage. Let us dig into this...

Your Notes . . .

What are the major causes of being Single today? Can these be prevented?

What are the ways to manage the crisis of being single?

The 3rd rd

MANAGING

CRISIS OF

CHOOSING IN

MARRIAGE

10. MANAGING CRISIS OF CHOOSING IN MARRIAGE···

MANAGING CRISIS OF CHOOSING IN MARRIAGE.

*I*n this chapter, we will be going through how to access your customised MARITAL MIRACLE in a step by step approach.

This exercise is an essential aspect of this book. As knowledge without application is not beneficial. In this session, we will be working with you as you translate the knowledge acquired into a fruitful application for a change of story for the better in your marriage.

The help of the Holy Ghost will aid this exercise. With GOD, all things are possible. If you are willing, you can access the customised miracle for your marriage.

MANAGING CRISIS IN CHOOSING FOR MARRIAGE!

NOW THAT I HAVE MADE A MISTAKE. WHAT IS NEXT?

Now that I made the wrong choice in marriage, what is next? What is the way out? This is our focus in this chapter.

We learnt the following at this stage:

1. Discover you before choosing!

2. The boundaries in choosing.

3. When to choose.

4. Engaging the divine helps.

5. And she said yes.

6. Introducing the Marital Monster

7. Being Single

We will now be looking into applications and lessons learnt to profer a way of escape through the help of the 3rd Person In Marriage: The HolySpirit.

POINTS OF RECORD.

- This book should be read together as a couple. However, even if you are alone in the journey of seeking your customized miracle or you are single preparing for your significant relationship. It is still okay. The 3rd Person is here to team with you.

- At the end of each chapter, we asked you to write down points you gained and how you wish to apply them; now is the time to use them.

- This exercise is a weekly plan; deeply looking into your life and your spouse's (if married) and seeing how much you align with the manual of marriage.

- You will be writing some notes, one for yourself and one for your spouse. and compare notes after (if you are already in a relationship). Or else, you do it solely for yourself if you are single.

- You may get a mentor or a supporting friend to support you during these exercises for accountability. All the very best!

- Be sincere as much as possible to get the best from these exercises. Remember, this is a good investment into your life and destiny. Great Grace, we pray in the Name of Yeshua Hamashiach (Jesus Christ), Amen.

WEEK 1.

1. DISCOVER YOU. BEFORE CHOOSING!

When you discover you first, making the right choice for marriage becomes easier. Beyond your natural temperaments, when you discover CHRIST, you will discover yourself.

Your Notes.

Who are you? Do you know?

What are the steps to take to discover your unique you?

Your Notes.

Did you discover yourself before choosing for Marriage?

If not, what are the deficits you now see in your Marriage due to this error in choosing? List them out.

Your Notes.

Will you be willing to let the 3rd Person in Marriage work with you and, for you, a customised way out of these problems? Because there is a way out!

How will you engage GOD to step into this area of your Marriage?

Share notes. Compare notes. Pray together.

Forgive all hurts.

Forgive misunderstandings.

Forgive the wrong background.

Forgive wrong assumptions.

Now, your spouse needs you. The 3rd Person in Marriage is ready to give you your customised miracles.

How much of the deficits can you tolerate? How much are you willing to change? How ready are you to allow the 3rd Person to fix you both? There is a CUSTOMISED MIRACLE for both of you. Seek for this. Pray for this, and you will experience it.

PRAYER POINTS.

Spend some time to pray together on your discoveries.

Commit your spouse unto the Lord, allowing the 3rd Person in Marriage, God, to help you and your spouse.

Thank God by faith for answers to prayers.

Write out your NEW and customised Marriage VALUES based on your situations and circumstances, letting God free hand to fix you both.

Congratulations.

WEEK 2.

2. THE BOUNDARIES IN CHOOSING.

Men are triune in nature.

You are a Spirit, you have a soul (will, mind and emotion), and you live in a body. Men tend to relate and operate at these three levels in making choices too.

As a believer, we are to choose primarily based on our Spiritual connectivity to CHRIST. Not just based on physical attractions or mental connectivity.

The Spirit rules. Hence a good character or physical endowment can be messed up by the Spiritual disposition.

Your Notes.

Why does one need boundaries in choosing for marriage? What are these boundaries?

Your Notes.

Now that one had chosen wrongly, what are some steps to birth a customized way out of the crisis?

Share notes. Compare notes. Pray together.

Forgive all hurts.

Forgive misunderstandings.

Forgive the wrong background.

Forgive wrong assumptions.

Now, your spouse needs you. The 3rd Person in Marriage is ready to give you your customised miracles.

How much of the deficits can you tolerate. How much are you willing to change. How ready are you to allow the 3rd Person in Marriage, God, to fix you both?

There is a CUSTOMISED MIRACLE for both of you. Seek for this. Pray for this, and you will experience it.

PRAYER POINTS.

Spend some time to pray together on your discoveries.

Commit your spouse unto the Lord, allowing the 3rd Person in Marriage, God, to help you and your spouse.

Thank God by faith for answers to prayers.

Write out your NEW and customised Marriage VALUES based on your situations and circumstances, letting God free hand to fix you both.

Congratulations.

WEEK 3.

3. WHEN TO CHOOSE.

Marriage is for all seasons. Hence choosing a life partner should not be at a season of life.

Discovering yourself, operating in the will of GOD and preparing oneself as a Godly man or woman for marriage are things to put in place before choosing for marriage!.

The question is, are you a Godly man yet? Do you possess the basic qualities of a Man? (1. Authority and dominion; 2. Vision and direction, and 3. Stability)

The boyish, the player, the confused, the Godly man; which one are you, dear brother?

Are you a Godly Woman yet? Do you possess the basic qualities of a woman? (1. Smartness and God-led intuition 2. Influence. 3. Beauty). Are they being expressed in offence or redemption?

Your Notes.

When is the right time to choose for marriage?

Your Notes.

What are the key purposes of life you should discover before choosing for marriage?

Share notes. Compare notes. Pray together.

Forgive all hurts.

Forgive misunderstandings.

Forgive the wrong background.

Forgive wrong assumptions.

Now, your spouse needs you. The 3rd Person in Marriage is ready to give you your customised miracles.

How much of the deficits can you tolerate. How much are you willing to change. How ready are you to allow the 3rd Person in Marriage, God, to fix you both?

There is a CUSTOMISED MIRACLE for both of you. Seek for this. Pray for this, and you will experience it.

PRAYER POINTS .

Spend some time to pray together on your discoveries.

Commit your spouse unto the Lord, allowing the 3rd Person in Marriage, God, to help you and your spouse.

Thank God by faith for answers to prayers.

Write out your NEW and customised Marriage VALUES based on your situations and circumstances, letting GOD free hand to fix you both.

Congratulations.

WEEK 4.

4. ENGAGING THE DIVINE HELPS.

Engaging the help of the Spirit, our divine helper here on earth, expressed mainly through the inner witness. (A simple, quiet, easy green light, leading you on or saying no). Very simple yet cannot be faked because it is sourced from your Spirit in union with CHRIST.

Engaging the divine helps through the local churches' marriage counselling committee—a great help platform.

Your Notes.

The Divine Helper: The HolySpirit. How will you engage Him in choosing for Marriage?

Your Notes.

The Divine Helper: Engaging the marriage counselling committees. What are their benefits in choosing for marriage?

Share notes. Compare notes. Pray together.

Forgive all hurts.

Forgive misunderstandings.

Forgive the wrong background.

Forgive wrong assumptions.

Now, your spouse needs you. The 3rd Person in Marriage is ready to give you your customised miracles.

How much of the deficits can you tolerate? How much are you willing to change? How ready are you to allow the 3rd Person to fix you both?

There is a CUSTOMISED MIRACLE for both of you. Seek for this. Pray for this, and you will experience it.

PRAYER POINTS.

Spend some time to pray together on your discoveries.

Commit your spouse unto the Lord, allowing the 3rd Person in Marriage, God, to help you and your spouse.

Thank God by faith for answers to prayers.

Write out your NEW and customised Marriage VALUES based on your situations and circumstances, letting God free hand to fix you both.

Congratulations.

WEEK 5.

5. AND SHE SAID YES.

The man in his God's given location, the woman, being positioned; and she said yes!

When a man is in his God's given location (will) and a woman is submitted to the Spirit of God to be well-positioned. Then she will be positioned near a man in his position and, Yes, She will!

Your Notes.

Man in his location, woman being positioned, and she said yes! What are your thoughts about this?

Share notes. Compare notes. Pray together.

Forgive all hurts.

Forgive misunderstandings.

Forgive the wrong background.

Forgive wrong assumptions.

Now, your spouse needs you. The 3rd Person in Marriage is ready to give you your customised miracles.

How much of the deficits can you tolerate? How much are you willing to change? How ready are you to allow the 3rd Person to fix you both?

There is a CUSTOMISED MIRACLE for both of you. Seek for this. Pray for this, and you will experience it.

PRAYER POINTS.

Spend some time to pray together on your discoveries.

Commit your spouse unto the Lord, allowing the 3rd Person in Marriage, God, to help you and your spouse.

Thank God by faith for answers to prayers.

Write out your NEW and customised Marriage VALUES based on your situations and circumstances, letting GOD free hand to fix you both.

Congratulations.

WEEK 6.

6. INTRODUCING THE MARITAL MONSTER.

The Marital Monster. The evil force that takes advantage of a compromised partner to oppress the other partner.

Your Notes.

The Marital Monster. Can you identify some of its striking characteristics?

Your Notes.

How can one overcome this evil force in our lives and that of our loved ones?

Share notes. Compare notes. Pray together.

Forgive all hurts.

Forgive misunderstandings.

Forgive the wrong background.

Forgive wrong assumptions.

Now, your spouse needs you. The 3rd Person in Marriage is ready to give you your customised miracles.

How much of the deficits can you tolerate? How much are you willing to change? How ready are you to allow the 3rd Person to fix you both?

There is a CUSTOMISED MIRACLE for both of you. Seek for this. Pray for this, and you will experience it.

PRAYER POINTS.

Spend some time to pray together on your discoveries.

Commit your spouse unto the Lord, allowing the 3rd Person in Marriage, God, to help you and your spouse.

Thank God by faith for answers to prayers.

Write out your NEW and customised Marriage VALUES based on your situations and circumstances, letting GOD free hand to fix you both.

Congratulations.

WEEK 7.

7. BEING SINGLE

Your Notes.

What are the major causes of being single today? Can they be prevented?

Your Notes.

What are the ways to manage the crisis of being single?

Share notes. Compare notes. Pray together.

Forgive all hurts.

Forgive misunderstandings.

Forgive the wrong background.

Forgive wrong assumptions.

Now, your spouse needs you. The 3rd Person in Marriage is ready to give you your customised miracles.

How much of the deficits can you tolerate? How much are you willing to change? How ready are you to allow the 3rd Person to fix you both?

There is a CUSTOMISED MIRACLE for both of you. Seek for this. Pray for this, and you will experience it.

PRAYER POINTS.

Spend some time to pray together on your discoveries.

Commit your spouse unto the Lord, allowing the 3rd Person in Marriage, God, to help you and your spouse.

Thank God by faith for answers to prayers.

Write out your NEW and customised Marriage VALUES based on your situations and circumstances, letting GOD free hand to fix you both.

Congratulations.

STUDY THIS TOGETHER.

MANAGING CRISIS AT THIS STAGE.

There is hope for wrong choices in marriage in Christ Jesus.

1. Repent, confess and return to GOD.

2. Accept and be willing to submit your will and marriage to GOD. Deciding to do it right this time!

3. Patiently follow as GOD turns things around in your favour:

- There may be a demand for some restitution.

- There may be some denials.

- There may be a long time of waiting.

The 3rd person in marriage (GOD) will give you a customized solution peculiar to your case in YESHUA HAMASHIACH's Name, Amen

Above all, remember that the enemy is targeting your salvation. Do not trade or lose your salvation because of marriage! Stick with Christ!

It is well in Yeshua Hamashiach's (Jesus Christ) Name, Amen

Share notes. Compare notes. Pray together.

Forgive all hurts.

Forgive misunderstandings.

Forgive the wrong background.

Forgive wrong assumptions.

Now, your spouse needs you. The 3rd Person in Marriage is ready to give you your customised miracles.

How much of the deficits can you tolerate? How much are you willing to change? How ready are you to allow the 3rd Person to fix you both?

There is a CUSTOMISED MIRACLE for both of you. Seek for this. Pray for this, and you will experience it.

PRAYER POINTS.

Spend some time to pray together on your discoveries.

Commit your spouse unto the Lord, allowing the 3rd Person in Marriage, God, to help you and your spouse.

Thank God by faith for answers to prayers.

Write out your NEW and customised EXPECTED QUALITIES for your Marriage, based on your situations and circumstances, while allowing GOD free hand to fix you both.

Congratulations.

If you follow these steps faithfully, just attempting it will endear you to your spouse if you are already in a relationship. Otherwise, it would have shed some light on some of the grey areas of your life and what you can improve upon while waiting for your Mr Right or Miss Right, if still single.

Like we said earlier. Marriage is a Miracle. There is a customized Miracle for your relationship based on your peculiarities. Deciding to allow the 3rd Person in Marriage to step in and take His rightful place is the main key to a Blissful Relationship.

And if you seem alone in the journey of creating your customized miracle, just do your part of the deal by aligning with the 3rd Person in Marriage. The two of you (GOD and You) are 'two agreeing together', which are enough to sort things out!

My dear friend, what will you rather do with this information? Will you like to share it with a friend that may appreciate it? Remember to keep your copy carefully. Let your friends get their copies.

. . . there are still more.

THE 3RD PERSON IN MARRIAGE SERIES...

When the Spirit of GOD nudged me to take on this series, I was super reluctant. who will not, for this was where I failed the most in my life -Marriage. (I thought!) However, right in the deepest valley of my failure, I encountered the 3rd Person in Marriage, who began to reveal step by step, precept upon precept, line upon line, how and why marriages fail, and why Marriage can be successful!

Like everything created and valued by GOD, the enemy attacks Marriage immensely at every stage of its life cycle. —The understanding stage (wrong perspective and beliefs on marriage); preparatory stage (wrong upbringing and abused childhood); choosing stage (wrong timing and choice of partners, or lack of partner); fusion stage (incompatibility at different levels); multiplication stage, (unfruitfulness physically, socially and spiritually); and reigning stage, (living in fulfilment in life).

This book series will show you WHY your marriage is working, so you might keep at it, or WHY it is not working, so you might see a customized way out for you.

Now that we have journeyed through the Choosing for Marriage. It is time to look into the other aspects of the marriage cycle. We pray they BLESS you too.

PREPARATIONS FOR MARRIAGE.

Preparations for Marriage. This book helps lay a solid foundation for Marriage, without which success is impossible. This volume addressed an in-depth understanding of marriage, the characteristics of the first man and woman, the 3rd person in marriage, preparing the boy and the girl for marriage, raising a Godly man and woman for marriage, and managing crisis due to abused, oppressed, and a poor foundation for marriage.

THE COMPATIBILITIES IN MARRIAGE.

The Compatibilities in Marriage. There are different levels of compatibilities with varied requirements. Many today tolerate their unions and live in hell daily because of compatibilities lacuna. This book focuses on compatibilities at different levels such as Physical, Mental, Spiritual, and Social compatibilities; Dealing with a gifted spouse and managing the crisis of compatibility In marriage. And how to avoid them.

MULTIPLICATIONS IN MARRIAGE.

The multiplications in Marriage. Not only is Marriage to be enjoyed, it is also expected to be fruitful. Can Marriage birth multiplications? Why is mine not? It focuses on Physical fruitfulness; Spiritual fruitfulness, Financial fruitfulness, Social fruitfulness, and managing the crisis of lack of multiplications in marriage.

REIGNING IN MARRIAGE.

The Reigning in Marriage. The original purpose of GOD creating man is to be fruitful, multiply, fill the earth, subdue and have dominion. This stage is expected to be reflected in marriage. This book focuses on enforcing Dominion in marriage; Invoking Generational BLESSING; Establishing the light that shines; Giving helping Hands to younger couples, and managing the crisis of reigning in marriage, among others.

PRAYER OF SALVATION···

Lord Jesus, I believe you are the SON of GOD that came to the world. You died on the cross for all Sins, Iniquities, and Transgressions. Your BLOOD redeemed man from all sins, and their consequences, from all curses, delivered man from the authority of darkness and translated them into your kingdom.

[11]I believe I, therefore, receive and confess you JESUS CHRIST as my Lord and Saviour. Thank you for dying for me and forgiven me of my sins. I receive by faith the forgiveness of my sins. I receive authority, the power to become a son of GOD, with the Gift of Righteousness, a Right Standing with GOD. I am delivered from Satan and all the forces of darkness. I am a new creature now; old things are passed away. Everything becomes new, thank you, Lord; I am born again. Amen. Alleluia.

Lord JESUS, you said you would send the HOLY SPIRIT to help us, teach us, comfort us, strengthen and reveal all truth to us. Now that I am born again, I ask by faith for the HOLY GHOST's Baptism in JESUS Name, Amen. Thank you because I have received HIM. Now, HE is mine; I give you GLORY, Amen. I speak by faith and trust that the HOLY SPIRIT gives me UTTERANCE now in JESUS NAME, AMEN.

---

[11] To contact us: Email: info@air.church

THANK YOU . . .

Thank you for reading this piece. We pray that it BLESSES you as it is BLESSING us too.

My dear friend, what will you rather do with this information?

Please share your experiences with us, email us at info@air.church and let us celebrate with you how this book has in any way helped in creating your customised marriage miracle. Thank you for the opportunity to share with you.

Expecting your testimonies. . .

Our GOD is GOOD, and HIS MERCIES endure forevermore, Amen.

pst tomowo
... setting men up with GOD, for a Glorious Turnaround.

some more ...

JESUS CHRIST... my Substitute, my Sacrifice, my Inheritance...

it starts with a substitution, followed by the sacrifice, then the inheritance. Until Christians lay hold on this truth, questions and doubts around the realities of CHRIST's existence and purpose for mankind will linger on . . ..

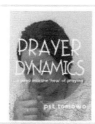

Prayer Dynamics

Many stumble on answers to prayers, and rejoices; however, due to a lack of understanding of the 'HOW' they got there, it becomes difficult to replicate the same again in future needs...You will create your own miracles through this...

THE SPIRIT REALM

In this world of uncertainties, answers are sought daily from many quarters... a peep into the spirit realm could clarify some of these qualms... what makes up the spirit realms, are there Anti-Christ in the world now, and the different kinds of churches today...

The LIFE Coaching ...

This is an online retreat, setting men up with GOD for a Glorious Turnaround. It is Flexible, self-paced.. at your leisure! It is customized to your needs and accessible on your mobile...It is fun while on retreat ...Yet, powerful to deliver your desired results.

*For more information on these ... Email us: **info@air.church**

Notes . . .

MEET PST TOMOWO.

'Tomowo Faduyile George (pst tomowo) is a passionate lover of GOD.

A dynamic and prophetic teacher of the WORD with a vivid presence of GOD's Anointing.

A trained pharmacist, expert in public health, a lover of people, team player, peace-loving, gentle and beautiful lady.

pst tomowo is called into teaching and ministering of GOD's GRACE, endowed with GOD's Presence, Power and Goodness.

She is known for her soft touch of motherly love, ready to Give, BLESS and Support. Having been through and overcome several long standing, life challenges, HELPED by GOD, pst tomowo pulls from this depth, always armed with a sweet smile and a word of encouragement for anyone that meets her, every time.

She is easily drawn to people in need, especially women, young adults and children.

She is a Life Coach, an author, artist, dynamic teacher of the Word, runs an all-online Faith based LIFE Coaching, accessible worldwide for retreats, self helps, mentoring and encounters for breakthrough... She also runs other online broadcasts...

Printed in Great Britain
by Amazon

85774997R00142